MOPO THE DAY!

Oggy Brewer

1 Cor 9:24

MOPO THE DAY!

Roger Bruner

1 Cor 9:24

MAX OUT PAY OUT

LIVING THE MOPO LIFE - MOPO THE DAY!

Oggy Brewer

WESTBOW
PRESS°
A DIVISION OF THOMAS NELSON
& ZONDERVAN

This book is a work of non-fiction. Unless otherwise noted, the author and the publisher make no explicit guarantees as to the accuracy of the information contained in this book and in some cases, names of people and places have been altered to protect their privacy.

WestBow Press books may be ordered through booksellers or by contacting:

WestBow Press
A Division of Thomas Nelson & Zondervan
1663 Liberty Drive
Bloomington, IN 47403
www.westbowpress.com
844-714-3454

Because of the dynamic nature of the Internet, any web addresses or links contained in this book may have changed since publication and may no longer be valid. The views expressed in this work are solely those of the author and do not necessarily reflect the views of the publisher, and the publisher hereby disclaims any responsibility for them.

Any people depicted in stock imagery provided by Getty Images are models, and such images are being used for illustrative purposes only.
Certain stock imagery © Getty Images.

Scripture quotations marked HCSB are taken from the Holman Christian Standard Bible®, Copyright © 1999, 2000, 2002, 2003, 2009 by Holman Bible Publishers. Used by permission. Holman Christian Standard Bible®, Holman CSB®, and HCSB® are federally registered trademarks of Holman Bible Publishers.

ISBN: 978-1-6642-2302-8 (sc)
ISBN: 978-1-6642-2301-1 (hc)
ISBN: 978-1-6642-2303-5 (e)

Library of Congress Control Number: 2021902826

Print information available on the last page.

WestBow Press rev. date: 02/17/2021

What in your life do you MAX OUT? Family Life? Work Life? School? Church? Sports? Vacation?

What do you want your PAY OUT to be? Building better relationships? Having a bigger paycheck? Growing with Christ? Your favorite TEAM winning a championship? Better Grades?

This book will challenge you to examine the things in your life you want to MAX OUT and to think about what you want your PAY OUT to be, blessing you with scripture to memorize and a MOPOLIFE quote to help you gain a better understanding of what it means to MOPO the DAY!

To the **Brew Crew** – our TEAM MOM – **Beth**
My big man in the paint – **Luke**
My power forward – **Olivia**
My point guard – **Mallory**
& My shooting guard – **Kellen**

Thank *you* for allowing me to live my best MOPO LIFE with you. Looking forward to many more MOPO DAYS together.

I had a vision. I wanted to get the most out of my life. I wanted to put my heart into the task at hand. I finished my basketball career (two years at Marian College and two years at Hanover College), graduated from Hanover, got married to Beth, got our first apartment together, and got my first job all in a matter of five months. Life was happening, and I had created a slogan for it: MOPO = MAX OUT PASS OUT.

I added to my vision. I was teaching and coaching at South Putnam Jr./Sr High School (four years) when my wife and I had our first child, Luke. I then moved on in my teaching/coaching career to Mooresville High School (fifteen years), and my wife and I had three more children during this time: Olivia, Mallory, & Kellen. MOPO = MAX OUT PASS OUT

My vision started to change. I decided to trademark MOPO, and it was during this time that I had been watching Shark Tank and got an idea. Knowing Mark Cuban is the owner of the Dallas Mavericks and an Indiana native, I decided to email him just to see what he thought about MOPO. To my surprise, Mark sent me an email back in a matter of fifteen minutes saying, "Don't know if we want to tell our kids to pass out, Oggy." These words got me thinking. *How could I change the meaning of MOPO?* After some thought, I created MOPO = MAX OUT PAY OUT!

My vision moving forward. With COVID-19 hitting hard and social/racial injustices going on, we need positive voices and positive experiences in our lives. As I thought back on my life and the positive voices in my ear as I grew up, the people who came to mind were my parents, teachers, youth ministers, and coaches. These people cheered me on, held me accountable, and helped me become who I am today. They were MAXING OUT in building relationships with me, and I am now benefiting from the PAY OUT.

I love sports — playing them, watching them, talking about them — and one of my favorite times of year is March Madness. I'm always intrigued by the team T-shirts players are wearing and would love to see them wearing MOPO MADNESS shirts as we watch the tournament unfold. Their daily challenges and ultimate goals align with what MOPO is all about.

Lastly, my ultimate vision is every person will experience living the MOPO LIFE. This book is full of Bible verses to help you in growing in the word and MOPO thoughts to help reinforce key focuses. This book will help you grow in your relationship with God and challenge you to invest in the lives of the people with whom you come into contact with each day: your family members, your neighbors, your co-workers, students or players, your church body, etc. Many are already doing so, but if you are not, here's to MAXING OUT your life so that you — along with others — will reap the PAY OUT!

FORWARD BY HANOVER
COACH JON MILLER

Today is September 15, 2020. About four months, at the start of many of the stay-at-home COVID-19 orders, my friend Matthew "Oggy" Brewer let me know he had set a goal for himself to write a book during the quarantine period. Here I am today with the pleasure of writing a foreword to that book. Over the past several years Oggy has consistently talked to me about the MOPO idea and it has become clear to me how much it means to him. I see it on his twitter and in his email signature. He gave me a baseball cap with a big MOPO on the front. The passion he has for the message has been clear for a while, and now him completing this book further illustrates his strong desire to share with others what he has found…the powerful message of MOPO – MAX OUT PAY OUT. I am honored to contribute a few pages to get it started.

I have known Oggy Brewer for over 35 years. His older brother Kyle was my best friend growing up on the southside of Indianapolis. Kyle and I went on to play 4 years of basketball together at Franklin Central HS and then another 4 years together at Hanover College. Like most younger brothers, Oggy would almost always tag along (as would my younger brother Michael) through summer days filled with whiffle ball games, 3v3 basketball in the driveway, and riding bikes to the local Village Pantry to buy baseball cards. Also like most younger brothers, Oggy often got the short end of the stick from his big brother – a close play at first always went Kyle's way, as did a foul on the driveway, and so too the Don Mattingly rookie card trade for three run-of-the-mill Reds outfielders. But even from the very beginning, one thing that was always certain about Oggy- he was always going to give his absolute best effort.

As Oggy grew older and bigger (6'5") I watched this determination to work and be the best he could be continue to grow. He went on to have a strong academic and basketball career at Franklin Central High School playing for head coach Mark James. Oggy (as was his brother Kyle) was really one of the poster guys for what Franklin Central Basketball stood for under Coach James. "Play Hard, Play Smart, Play Together." A collection of guys willing to work hard and together in order to reach their full potential. 3 hour practices, 12-month a year weight lifting, and every weekday of the summer meant 8AM shooting workouts and 7:30PM open gym. One of the more common phrases we would hear would be, "What you give is yours, what you don't is lost forever." (This might have originated from State Championship football coach Chuck Stephens.)

After high school in the fall of 1998 Oggy decided to attend Marian University to study and play basketball. For me, during this time I had graduated from college and started in on a career in college coaching. I started out for a couple of years as a graduate assistant coach at DePauw University (1997-99) and then was hired back at Hanover College as the full-time assistant coach in 1999. By the end of Oggy's sophomore year at Marian, in the summer of 2000, I was engaged to be married. The Brewer family (led by Rick "The Rocket" Brewer) hosted a cookout/party at their house for me on a Saturday that June. All of Kyle and my Hanover teammates were there as well as my brother and of course Oggy. It just so happened that as we were all hanging out, Oggy and I got to talking and joking that maybe he should come to Hanover to play his final 2 years. I am not sure either of us took the conversation all that seriously, but one thing led to another and by the middle of August Oggy had enrolled at Hanover. (*Funny side note, Oggy is my one-and-only NCAA recruiting violation. It turns out that Marian was not too happy about him transferring so they called the NCAA. Our informal conversation at the cookout in June was considered outside the rules since it was prior to us having an official release! Luckily both Hanover and the NCAA were fairly understanding of the situation but I did receive a formal reprimand!)

So for the 2000-01 and 2001-02 seasons Oggy was a player at Hanover, under Head Coach Mike Beitzel, while I was the assistant coach. Og joined a great group of guys at Hanover – several who have gone on to become Indiana HS basketball coaches. It was a hard-working, team-first group already, but adding Oggy made it even more that way. You never had to coach Og's effort. He might have been a little too slow to at times "Reach-step" and stay in front of the ball on defense, but it was never for a lack of effort. He was a guy that gave you everything he had on every play. Beyond his effort, Oggy was a complete team guy. He was always most interested in the success of the team and was willing to put all his effort in making that his top priority.

As I think back over Oggy's Hanover playing career, there was a time I remember specifically one spring afternoon. It was a day after the team had worked out and the other guys had left the gym. Og and I were talking and he stated that he just could not understand why some of the younger guys on the team were not motivated to consistently work as hard as they could. Why they "took some days off." Why they didn't understand that the opportunity to play basketball would not last forever and that because of this it made sense that you should take full advantage of every day. I remember telling him that I thought this reality would be one of the biggest challenges and opportunities as he entered a career in coaching -understanding that not many guys would have his level of internal drive but then also trying to help them in this area.

As I write this foreword to Oggy's MOPO (Max Out Pay Out) book I can't help but think back to that conversation. While I know Og has shared the same frustrations we all have from time to time during his coaching career, his development of the concept of MOPO is his heart-felt attempt at a sharing a solution as opposed to only complaining. I admire his passion (and hope you will too) for MOPO and for desire to sharing these thoughts and the thoughts of others in a book, intended to help motivate them to be all they can be and give all they can give in areas of their lives.

For me personally, as I enter my 18th year as a small college head coach, and 13th year as the head coach at Hanover College (IN) I have learned that the concept of MOPO can be a tremendous strategy for finding success. In life we are all looking for things that are GUARANTEED - if we fully commit to them then success is certain to follow. However when we are honest, we know that very few of these guaranteed returns actually exist. This is the beauty of MOPO – I have found that it can certainly come with that guarantee we are looking for if we approach it correctly. We are all guaranteed a PAY OUT if we are willing to truly MAX OUT. I'll use my group of players at Hanover each year as an example.

As each school year begins, and we get all our returning players and new freshmen together, I tell our guys that our #1 goal needs to be to have a TEAM. It sounds simple, but I am talking about intently working to become a group of guys who have a genuine love and affection for each other. A group who develops in a way that it eventually derives more satisfaction from TEAM or TEAMmate success than any individual accolade of their own. One of the reasons, but not the only reason, we work to be a TEAM is that we believe being a TEAM maximizes our chance to win a championship. Certainly, a championship won by a TEAM is the ultimate team PAY OUT. But I have found that if we build a TEAM, even in years we come up short on a championship – there is <u>always</u> a PAY OUT. There is a satisfaction that comes from working your hardest, MAXING OUT, with your TEAMmates that can never be taken away no matter the final score of the final game. I have found MOPO is very similar to Coach Wooden's thought on how self-satisfaction (PAY OUT) is a direct result of knowing you did your best (MAX OUT) to become the best you were capable of becoming.

Oggy has done a great job of pulling together people from all walks of life in this book, as MOPO can cross about any boundary and translate into every situation. It can be both personal and professional. For myself as a coach, and I bet a lot of other highly-driven people in their profession, if we are honest we know there are times we need to press the pause button and find a little better focus on our personal MOPO. Personally, I have found it is not always easy, the Max Out part is always a decision and sometimes that decision is easier to make than others. But when we get that MAX OUT right, the PAY OUT is always there. As a husband, father, Christian, coach, friend the times I am most intentional in my MAX OUT, the PAY OUT is the greatest. The result isn't the guarantee, but the absolute satisfaction and peace of mind that comes from knowing you MAXED OUT is a constant.

I hope that you will enjoy this book as much as I have. And more than that I hope that we all can all find areas and make decisions to MAX OUT just a little more often. In the words of Oggy Brewer, *"MOPO the DAY!"*

MOPO Coaching

Coach Miller was my assistant Basketball Coach at Hanover when I played (2000-2002).

He is coaching his 13th season as the Head Coach of the Panthers.

MOPO License Plate

If you see this license plate on the road, it's a great reminder to - MOPO the Day😊!

Max Out Pay Out

LIVING THE MOPO LIFE

"Do you not know that the runners in a stadium all race, but only one receives the prize? Run in such a way that you may win."

1 Corinthians 9:24

We live in a fast-paced, activity-driven, sports-crazed, on-the-go world. Our schedules are filled to the *MAX* with school activities, competitions, vacations, Little League sports, church meetings, and work. We are a society on the move. We are a society living in fear, shame, guilt, anxiety, and worry. We allow the negativity of the day to keep us from seizing an abundant life. The MOPO LIFE represents running the race to *WIN*. The MOPO LIFE is living a life where we don't let our doubts overcome our faith. We stretch ourselves and recognize that no matter what is happening in our world, we have faith in knowing that God is still on the throne.

I grew up in a small town in Indiana called Wanamaker. I had two loving, supportive parents, Rick and Sara Brewer. My dad was a teacher/coach/AD at Franklin Township Middle School. My mom worked different jobs while staying at home to raise my older brother, Kyle, my younger sister, Brittany and me. We lived in a small, three-bedroom home that did not have an air conditioner. To keep cool during those hot summer months, we would run fans in each window. Kyle and I shared a bunk bed during most of my younger years. It was in these years, that the foundation of living out the MOPO LIFE was being built.

I was a go-with-the-flow type of kid who had a love for life. My parents instilled in me at a young age to always give my best, work hard, and be honest. These are traits I continue to try to live by today. In living out these traits, I learned

1

that when I committed myself to something, I was all in. For example, my dad introduced us to the *Rocky* movies and would always exercise in a hat, sweatpants, and sweatshirt no matter the temperature outside. It allowed for extra pounds to be shed but also was for an added mental edge. If I could make the exercise a little more challenging and get through it, I knew I could fight through just about anything. It was the Rocky mentality: "It's not about how hard you hit; it's about how hard you can get hit and keep moving forward — how much you can take and keep moving forward. That's how winning is done!" This had an impact on me in my youth and had carryover to my adult life. To this day, I continue to wear a hat, a sweatshirt, and sweatpants to exercise and workout. I'm all in. That's the MOPO ATTITUDE!

As I continued to grow up, I watched as my dad became Athletic Director at Franklin Township Middle School, where my brother, sister, and I would attend. It was here I witnessed the importance of building positive relationships. As a new sports season started, coaches would make their way to my dad's office where he would provide the best coaching gear to show support to his coaches. Although I didn't fully understand it at the time, my dad was teaching me the value of building positive relationships with co-workers. Put value in the people who work for you. Care for the people who are in your life. It's another part of the MOPO ATTITUDE.

Looking back on my life, my parents were giving me life experiences to help mold and shape me into who I am today. They actively modeled the importance of showing unconditional love and holding yourself accountable. My parents weren't the only transformational leaders in my life. There were numerous teachers, coaches, and family friends who guided me, challenged me, held me accountable, and helped shape my faith. Their impact is reflected in part on the following pages. In reading this book, you will be reminded that in your role as a parent, teacher, coach, or family friend, you can impact the people who are in your life while also growing in your own. It will be in this growth of building relationships that you will be living out the MOPO LIFE.

While this book will explain the MOPO LIFE, it is my goal to help spread the Gospel and help bring hope in a time of struggle. May God be glorified and your soul be stirred as you read this book. Enjoy!

MOPO THE DAY!

<u>MOPO Family</u>

Smiles all around. Not sure what the photographer said, but it sure got me laughing in this picture.

Good reminder, that when you MOPO - keep perspective - make sure you have laughter in your day.

MOPO STORY

He was a walk-on football player at a highly prestigious university. Coaches would describe him as a hard worker, disciplined in all aspects of his life, and a great TEAMMATE. His colorful personality added to the room. He was one of the first to show up for practices and one of the last to leave. He was a highly motivated individual, who got the most out of his ability.

Today he would be rewarded for all of his hard work throughout the years - - a full ride scholarship.

"I'm *all* In." What are the things in your life where you can answer, "I'm *all* in?" In your family life? In your work place? In your Christian walk? With your friends? In your prayer life? When you are trying to exercise and lose weight? When you say the words, "I'm *all* in," you bring an enthusiasm and an attitude that shows you are a force to be reckoned with. You set a standard for yourself to show up and bring your best effort. When you answer with the words, "I'm *all* in," you are on your way to the start of Living the MOPO LIFE. What is the MOPO LIFE? The MOPO LIFE is living your best life each day. The goal of MOPO is to start each day with a thankful heart, knowing you have been blessed with a new day and new opportunity to take on with a positive attitude whatever the day brings. At the end of the day, you can be content in giving your best effort. The MOPO LIFE represents living freely in Christ.

MOPO stands for **M**AX **O**UT **P**AY **O**UT. When you are living life and **M**AXING **O**UT each day with your best effort, there will be a **P**AY **O**UT for you. This can apply to many things in life:

> Your Family – As a father/mother, when you spend time with your kids (**M**AX **O**UT) and really support them. Your **P**AY **O**UT will be growing in your relationship with them and seeing your kids thrive and make the most of their lives.

> Your Work – Giving your best each day at work (**M**AX **O**UT) will result in an actual pay check for you (**P**AY **O**UT). Hopefully, it will also result in growing relationships and having an impact on others (**P**AY **O**UT).

> Teaching/Coaching- Being prepared with a plan each day and carrying out your plan (**M**AX **O**UT) with your student-athletes will result in a **P**AY **O**UT. They will improve and grow in their class/sport.

> Sports – Playing sports brings on many opportunities to compete, to build relationships, and to grow in your craft (**M**AX **O**UT). The **P**AY **O**UT can be winning a big game, forming a lifelong

friendship, or living with the satisfaction that you have given your all.

Exercise – Taking time to stay active — walking, jogging, biking, or using an elliptical (**M**AX **O**UT) — will result in a **P**AY **O**UT of being in better physical shape and better mental toughness.

Walk with Christ – When you spend time in prayer, reading your Bible, memorizing scripture, and serving (**M**AX **O**UT), your **P**AY **O**UT will be growing in Christ and being closer to Him.

Relationships – Investing in relationships and taking time to really get to know people (**M**AX **O**UT) will result in deeper bonds and friendships formed (**P**AY **O**UT).

MOPO also stands for **M**AX **O**UT **P**ASS **O**UT. This can apply in a few areas of your life:

Raising Kids - As a father of four kiddos, I understand the ups and downs of parenting. I continue to learn. There are some days you struggle to survive. When your six-month old doesn't know their days from their nights, you might be ready to pull your hair out at three o'clock in the morning. You are in survival mode. You are **M**AXING **O**UT and your body is ready to **P**ASS **O**UT.

Your Worries & Anxieties - The goal here is to **M**AX **O**UT your positive thoughts and to **P**ASS **O**UT your negative ones. By keeping your thoughts on things of significance, it will allow you to live out your best MOPO LIFE.

This book is designed to have a positive influence on your day. It is filled with thoughts on the MOPO LIFE and Bible verses to sew in your hearts. While not every Bible verse relates directly to the MOPO LIFE saying, there is wisdom in each verse. One challenge I would give you is to memorize the verse for each day. Write it down, put it on your mirror, and interact with it. As you do this, you will continue down the road of your best MOPO LIFE.

The book is also sprinkled with everyday people — coaches, teachers, administrators, and ministers — and their thoughts on LIVING OUT the MOPO LIFE.

MOPO STORY

He and his wife had known each other for 50 years. They had met in high school and had never separated from each other. They married right out of college and started a family together. With four grown kids, many memories made, and lots of plans for retirement, she got cancer. Their world was turned upside down. He grabbed her hand, said a prayer, and told her, "We will get through this as we've done everything else in this life - - with God's help and together."

MOPO THE DAY!

TESTIMONIALS

"I am learning to MAX OUT my understanding that my identity is not something I do or accomplish, but has been given to me by my Creator. The PAY OUT is a freedom and fulfillment that allows me to enjoy coaching beyond any success or failure that comes with the game."

Greg Tonagel, Indiana Wesleyan University – Men's Basketball Coach

"I have always been taught to serve others & in my role as an athletic director I am given the opportunity to serve coaches, faculty, & students on a daily basis. We are immersed in a society where it is all about "ME" & Christ makes it clear that we are to strive to serve others in all we say & do. The opportunity to be a part of a student's "college journey" is a blessing to see a life changed & a young adult who is ready to tackle the world for Christ & impact society. May we always take the path less traveled!"

Chad Briscoe, Grace College Athletic Director

"One of the challenges for me as a coach in our competitive work-space, is to find a good balance & make sure my MAX OUT as a coach does not take away from my MAX OUT as a husband & dad. The biggest thing I try to MAX OUT in my life is my time. Create enough quality & quantity of time for my wife, my kids, & for my God. Try to not be distracted by other things when having that time. I know I come up short at times in this area, but when I get it right - - the PAY OUT is great! A feeling that my priorities are in line & a stronger, closer relationship with my wife, my kids, & the Lord."

Jon Miller, Hanover College Men's Basketball Coach

LIVING YOUR BEST MOPO LIFE

Every day is an adventure. One of the things I enjoy most about teaching and coaching is knowing I get an opportunity to have an impact on the kids I see each day. I get to form relationships, be a role model, speak wisdom, pray for the kids, watch them mature over the course of the year, and then see them as they pursue life after high school. I get to have an impact. Whether at home, school, or work, every day brings on its own challenge. I've learned throughout my life the importance of the following things:

FOLLOWING GOD'S SPIRIT: When we accept Jesus as our Lord & Savior, God gives us the gift of the Holy Spirit. The Holy Spirit will direct your path if you take the time to listen and be in tune with God.

> **SHOWING UP:** Most times the battle is getting yourself motivated to get out of bed and get the day started. Showing up is the first step.

> **BEING PRESENT:** Being present means giving your full attention to the task at hand. That means putting the cell phone down.

> **GIVING YOUR BEST EFFORT**: You don't have to be the smartest, fastest, strongest, most athletic person to give your best; it's an attitude of knowing each day you gave it your all.

> **WORKING HARD**: Put on your hardhat and go to work. Each of us is given an opportunity to work, so we should approach each

task knowing we will put forth the effort needed to get the job done right.

SHOW CARE FOR OTHERS: People matter. The people in your world matter. A lot can be said about your character with how you interact with the people you come into contact with every day. Taking time to say hello or ask how a neighbor is doing can go a long way in a growing a positive relationship. Be respectful of the people in your life.

BEING COACHABLE: Whether you are listening to your boss, a teacher, a coach, a friend, or your husband/wife, each of us needs to be humble and do the things being asked of us without complaining. We need to trust the people over us.

BEING HONEST: There is peace in always giving an honest answer — letting your YES be YES and your NO be NO. People can trust the things you say.

By **MAXING OUT** in each of these areas, you give yourself an opportunity every day to MOPO the DAY! Every day offers an opportunity to **MAX OUT**, and as we **MAX OUT**, a **PAY OUT** will form. The **PAY OUT** can range from having satisfaction of a job well done — to making money, to losing weight, to growing deeper in relationship, to winning a championship.

It is up to you to decide how you will **MAX OUT** your day and what you would like your **PAY OUT** to be. It is my challenge that as you think about and answer those questions, you will be on your way to LIVING YOUR BEST MOPO LIFE!

There are several things you can do to MO (**MAX OUT**) in the MOPO (**MAX OUT PAY OUT**) LIFE:

o   Wake up each day with a thankful and humble heart.
o   Give your best effort in all you do.
o   Work hard.

o   Trust the people in your life.
o   Be willing to serve, and be a good friend.
o   Read your Bible and pray. Yield and allow yourself to grow in your relationship with God.

By **M**AXING **O**UT in these areas, there are many ways you get a PO (**P**AY **O**UT) in the MOPO (**M**AX **O**UT **P**AY **O**UT) LIFE:

o   You are mentally ready to start each day with an overload of optimism.
o   You can accomplish a goal that was set.
o   You can be a better spouse, father/mother, friend, and or colleague.
o   You can build lifelong relationships.
o   You can get peace of mind and satisfaction in knowing you've done your best and given your all.
o   You can grow in your relationship with Christ.

What do I want to **M**AX **O**UT in my personal life? In my work life?

_____

_____

What do I want the **P**AY **O**UT to be in my personal life? In my work life?

_____

_____

What is one area I want to improve in (Being present, giving my best, working hard, or being coachable)?

_____

_____

List 2 MOPO (**M**AX **O**UT **P**AY **O**UT) goals for your life.

_____

_____

Describe what LIVING YOUR BEST MOPO LIFE means to you.

_____

_____

MOPO LIFE: IT'S ABOUT MAXING OUT EVERYTHING YOU DO. MOPO THE DAY!

Proverbs 4:23

Guard your heart above all else,
For it is the source of life.

MOPO LIFE: IT'S GOING THE EXTRA MILE. MOPO THE DAY!

Matthew 23:11-12

Jesus said, "The greatest among you will be your servant. Whoever exalts himself will be humbled, and whoever humbles himself will be exalted."

MOPO LIFE: IT'S ABOUT ENJOYING THE JOURNEY. MOPO THE DAY!

Proverbs 3:5-6

Trust in the Lord with all your heart,
And do not rely on your own understanding;

Think about Him in all your ways,
And He will guide you on the right paths.

MOPO LIFE: IT'S DOING THINGS THE RIGHT WAY . . . ALL THE TIME. MOPO THE DAY!

Proverbs 4:24

Don't let your mouth speak dishonestly,
& don't let your lips talk deviously.

MOPO LIFE: IT'S MAKING TIME FOR YOUR FAMILY. MOPO THE DAY!

Proverbs 22:6

Teach a youth about the way he should go;
Even when he is old he will not depart from it.

MOPO LIFE: IT'S MAKING TIME FOR YOUR FRIENDS. MOPO THE DAY!

Proverbs 15:7

When a man's ways please the Lord,
He makes even his enemies to be at peace with Him.

MOPO LIFE: IT'S FRIDAY! MOPO THE DAY!

Proverbs 4:26

Carefully consider the path for your feet,
And all your ways will be established.

MOPO LIFE: IT'S WALKING OUTSIDE TO TEMPERATURES IN THE 30'S WITHOUT YOUR JACKET. MOPO THE DAY!

Proverbs 6:6

Go to the ant, you slacker!
Observe its ways and become wise.

MOPO LIFE: IT'S DRINKING THAT 4TH CUP OF COFFEE ON A MONDAY MORNING. MOPO THE DAY!

Proverbs 14:2

Whoever lives with integrity fears the Lord,
But the one who is devious in his ways despises Him.

MOPO LIFE: IT'S BEING KIND. MOPO THE DAY!

Proverbs 17:17

A friend loves at all times,
And a brother is born for a difficult time.

MOPO LIFE: IT'S TAKING TIME TO LOOK UP - - DON'T MISS THE SUN SHINING, THE STARS, OR THE NATURE ALL AROUND YOU. MOPO THE DAY!

Matthew 24:42-44

Jesus said, "Therefore be alert, since you don't know what day your Lord is coming. But know this: If the homeowner had known what time the thief was coming, he would have stayed alert & not let his house be broken into. This is why you also must be ready, because the Son of Man is coming at an hour you do not expect."

MOPO LIFE: IT'S TAKING TIME TO LISTEN - - GOD GAVE YOU TWO EARS & ONE MOUTH FOR A REASON. MOPO THE DAY!

Ephesians 4:15

But speaking the truth in love, let us grow in every way into Him who is the head—Christ.

MOPO LIFE: IT'S TAKING A BREATH - - SLOW DOWN - - STOP! BE THANKFUL FOR THE DAY! MOPO THE DAY!

Proverbs 15:18

A hot-tempered man stirs up conflict,
But a man slow to anger calms strife.

MOPO LIFE: IT'S GOING ALL IN! ALL IN ON . . . HOW HARD YOU PLAY . . . HOW YOU LOVE YOUR FAMILY . . . HOW YOU DO YOUR JOB . . . HOW YOU WORSHIP . . . HOW YOU LIVE OUT YOUR LIFE. MOPO THE DAY!

Psalm 95:1-2

Come, let us shout joyfully to the Lord, shout triumphantly to the rock of our salvation! Let us enter His presence with thanksgiving; let us shout triumphantly to Him in song.

Verses 6-7

Come let us worship & bow down; let us kneel before the Lord our Maker. For He is our God, & we are the people of His pasture, the sheep under His care.

MOPO LIFE: IT'S LOVING OTHERS. MOPO THE DAY!

John 15:12-14

Jesus said, "This is My command: love one another as I have loved you. No one has greater love than this, that someone would lay down his life for his friends. You are My friends if you do what I command you."

MOPO STORY

He had served faithfully for 60 years. He raised three kids, was able to build a strong relationship with eight grandkids, and was enjoying the fruits of meeting two great-grandkids. He had served many roles in the church, including eldership for fifteen years. He tried to pursue love, righteousness, gentleness, and peacefulness — all with a faithful spirit. He modeled forgiveness and kindness to all and brought many to know Jesus. At the end of his life, he left a legacy in which the family could lean on and try to model at the same time. He endured the race with faithfulness, and now it was time for God to speak: "Well done, good and faithful servant!"

MOPO THE DAY!

MOPO Coaching Experience

The Mooresville Basketball Coaching Staff led by Coach Bob Carter got to watch the #1 ranked Indiana Hoosiers at the time, practice at Assembly Hall. Taking coaching trips to see how other programs put in the work is a great MOPO Coaching Experience. MOPO the Day!

TESTIMONIALS

"I love to see our students MAX OUT the high school experience. When they truly engage in groups, teams, & other organizations they are building confidence, leadership, & learning lessons they can not learn in the classroom. Whether it is performing arts, sports, academic teams, or any other activity it is extremely valuable. All of those life lessons are invaluable."

Steve Ahaus, Franklin Community High School Principal

"I hope that our athletes will MAX OUT modeling empathy, humility, integrity, work ethic and that they will be a good teammate. If our athletes model these things while they walk the halls of Mooresville High School I am confident that the PAY OUT will be responsible coworkers, community leaders, spouses and parents.

Mike Mossbrucker, Mooresville High School Athletic Director

"We try to MAX OUT four principles for success in our program: Competing, Being a Great Teammate, Being Coachable, & Accepting Your Role and Playing it to the Maximum of Your Ability."

**Scott McClelland, Morristown Boys Varsity
Basketball Coach; 226 Career WINS**

"I want to MAX OUT loving God with all my heart, soul, mind, & strength on a daily basis. My PAY OUT will be a growing relationship with Jesus."

Becky Kenworthy, CPA

"I MAX OUT in my life by realizing the best is yet to come. The PAY OUT is eternity with loved ones & Jesus."

Sara Brewer, Best MOM in the World – My Mom

MOPO THE DAY

Each day is a blessing. Every day we get an opportunity to MOPO (**M**AX **O**UT **P**AY **O**UT) the Day. What does that mean? You get an opportunity to get the most out of your day. What is your plan for the day? Are you going to attack the day? How are you going to approach your work, your family, and your free time? Are you going to help someone today? Take a look at your agenda, and make the best of what you are doing for the day.

MOPO the Day means you are going to know that no matter what comes your way, God is in control. I like to start my day with a reading of God's word and some prayer time. I'm going to welcome God into my day and each thing I have planned for that day. I will ask for His protective hand over me and my family and ask for my spirit to be in tune with His. In my conversation with God, I tell Him that I want to live for Christ and ask for His Spirit to guide me throughout my day. I ask God for His blessing on the day.

MOPO the Day means I'm going to have a positive perspective on the day. I get to start a new day with a clean slate. What will I do with my day? Give my best, see the best in people, serve people, and work hard to be at my best. I'm excited about the new day, and I'm thankful God has blessed me with it. I don't want to waste it.

MOPO stands for **M**AX **O**UT **P**AY **O**UT. This means you are going to **M**AX **O**UT your day – give your all – so at the end of the day it will **P**AY **O**UT.

The MO (**M**AX **O**UT) in the MOPO (**M**AX **O**UT **P**AY **O**UT) Experience of your DAY is...

- o waking up in the morning with a positive perspective on the day.
- o getting on your knees to lift the day up to the Lord.
- o being willing to listen to the Spirit and do the things being stirred in your heart.
- o seeing the best in people daily.
- o living out the day: making sure you laugh, you love, and you bring light to the world.

The PO (**P**AY **O**UT) in the MOPO (**M**AX **O**UT **P**AY **O**UT) Experience of your DAY is...

- o having a healthier mental and physical attitude.
- o growing in your walk with Christ as you see the fruits of the Spirit in your life: love, joy, peace, patience, kindness, goodness, faith, gentleness, and self-control.
- o finding more enjoyment in the people and challenges that are in your life.
- o building better relationships with the people in your life.

What is your best day?

Example: Get up early, have quiet time with the Lord, Exercise, Go to Work, Come home – spend time with your family, Dinner around the table, Watch a movie, Bed time

Example: Wake up to the sunrise, Walk the beach, Swim in the ocean, Soak up the sun, Dinner at a nice restaurant with your significant other

Example: Wake up to donuts & milk, Go to the Super Bowl - - your TEAM WINS, Celebrate with friends

If you were to write down what your best MOPO (MAX OUT PAY OUT) day looks like, what would it be?

_____

_____

Understandably, you can't go to the Super Bowl every day, but you can MOPO each day!

Write out how you will MOPO this DAY? MAX OUT THE DAY!

_____

_____

I would like to challenge you to live it out = MOPO the Day!

MOPO LIFE: IT'S BEING AN ENCOURAGER. BE SUPPORTIVE. BE KIND. BE A FRIEND. MOPO THE DAY!

Proverbs 27:9

Sweet friendships refresh the soul and awaken our hearts with joy, for good friends are like the anointing oil that yields the fragrant incense of God's presence.

MOPO LIFE: IT'S MAKING SURE YOU LAUGH TODAY. MOPO THE DAY!

Job 8:21

He will yet fill your mouth with laughter & your lips with a shout of joy.

MOPO LIFE: IT'S NEVER GIVING UP. MOPO THE DAY!

2 Corinthians 4:16-18

Therefore we do not give up; even though our outer person is being destroyed, our inner person is being renewed day by day.

MOPO LIFE: IT'S WORKING HARD & STAYING THE COURSE. MOPO THE DAY!

Proverbs 21:3

Doing what is righteous and just
Is more acceptable to the Lord than sacrifice.

MOPO LIFE: IT'S HAVING A DRINK WITH AN OLD FRIEND & RELIVING THE GOOD OLD DAYS. MOPO THE DAY!

Psalm 90:14

Satisfy us in the morning with Your faithful love so that we may shout with joy & be glad all our days.

MOPO LIFE: IT'S MAKING OUT WITH THE LOVE OF YOUR LIFE UNDER THE STARS. MOPO THE DAY!

Song of Songs 1:2

Oh, that he would kiss me with the kisses of his mouth! For your love is more delightful than wine.

MOPO LIFE: IT'S BUYING YOUR FIRST CAR & KEEPING IT SHINY FOR DAYS. MOPO THE DAY!

Psalm 62:5-6

Rest in God alone, my soul, for my hope comes from Him.
He alone is my rock & my salvation, my stronghold; I will not be shaken.

MOPO LIFE: IT'S GETTING CAUGHT UP IN A GOOD BOOK. MOPO THE DAY!

Psalm 143:8

Let me experience Your faithful love in the morning, for I trust in You.
Reveal to me the way I should go, because I long for You.

MOPO LIFE: IT'S BENGE WATCHING YOUR FAVORITE NETFLIX SHOW. MOPO THE DAY!

Psalm 27:4

I have asked one thing from the Lord;

It is what I desire: to dwell in the house of the Lord all the days of my life, gazing on the beauty of the Lord & seeking Him in His temple.

MOPO LIFE: IT'S TURNING ON THE RADIO TO YOUR FAVORITE SONG PLAYING. MOPO THE DAY!

1 John 1:9

If we confess our sins, He is faithful & righteous to forgive us our sins & to cleanse us from all unrighteousness.

MOPO LIFE: IT'S THE SMELL OF FRESHLY CUT GRASS. MOPO THE DAY!

Luke 6:43-44

Jesus said, "A good tree doesn't produce bad fruit; on the other hand, a bad tree doesn't produce good fruit. For each tree is known by its own fruit.

MOPO LIFE: IT'S TAKING A LONG BIKE RIDE WITH YOUR FRIENDS AND COASTING DOWN THE HILL. MOPO THE DAY!

Psalm 57:9-11

I will praise You, Lord, among the peoples; I will sing praises to You among the nations.
For Your faithful love is as high as the heavens;
Your faithfulness reaches the clouds.
God, be exalted above the heavens;
Let Your glory be over the whole earth.

MOPO LIFE: IT'S TAKING A NAP ON A SUNDAY AFTERNOON. MOPO THE DAY!

Deuteronomy 5:12-14

Be careful to dedicate the Sabbath day, as the Lord your God has commanded you. You are to labor six days & do all your work, but the seventh day is a Sabbath to the Lord your God. You must not do any work - - you, your son or daughter, your male or female slave your ox or donkey, any of your livestock, or the foreigner who lives within your gates, so that your male & female slaves may rest as you do.

MOPO LIFE: IT'S MAKING A NEW FRIEND. MOPO THE DAY!

Ecclesiastes 4:9-12

Two are better than one because they have a good reward for their efforts. For if either falls, his companion can lift him up; but pity the one who falls without another to lift him up. Also, if two lie down together, they can keep warm; but how can one person alone keep warm? And if somebody overpowers one person, two can resist him. A cord of three strands is not easily broken.

MOPO LIFE: IT'S DANCING EVERY CHANCE YOU GET. MOPO THE DAY!

Psalm 150:4

Praise Him with tambourine and dance;
Praise Him with flute and strings.

MOPO STORY

He had been in coaching for almost 40 years. He had developed a winning system that taught the fundamentals of the game. His program would be described as having players who worked hard, were disciplined, and competed well. His players learned how to become great TEAMMATES, respected the game and the coach, played for more than the name on the back of their jersey, and competed at a high level.

After graduation, one player got hired for a great company, got married, and started a family. The first time the player had to get up at 2:30 in the morning to take care of the baby, he realized all the discipline it took to get to early morning workouts had prepared him for these moments of fatherhood.

His coach was teaching more than just the game.

MOPO THE DAY!

TESTIMONIALS

"I MAX OUT as a father by giving my time to my kids = Intentional, Present TIME. The PAY OUT is trust & a closer relationship with them. Another PAY OUT is joy - - in laughter; in deep conversations & in hearing their heart."

Andy Lynch, Outreach Minister

"Sometimes, MAXING OUT as a dad can be as simple as "being present" for our kids. There was a time in my life when I had to spend some time away from my family at a rehab facility. I had become addicted to my pain pills & I couldn't get clean on my own. I left for a month & was able to detox & begin my road to recovery. While I'm thankful for my time there & the freedom I discovered, as you can imagine I went through some pretty low periods as well. I missed my wife. I missed my kids. During one of those low moments I shared my regrets with one of my counselors. I asked him what I should do as a father when I returned home (I wanted to make up for lost time.) What should I say? Where should I take them? What should I do? I'll never forget his answer. He said, "Just BE PRESENT." Be present. Sounds simple, but it stuck with me. So often (whether we're addicted to drugs or alcohol, or whether it's something less dramatic like becoming preoccupied with work when you're home at night or engaged in the latest ball game on TV instead of playing catch in the backyard), the greatest thing we can do to MAX OUT as a father is to be present. Turn off the TV, make their ballgames a priority, shut off Facebook. Choose to be present & live in the moment with your kids, & the PAY OUT will be deepening relationships, a spirit of love & connection, & trust built between you & the people you cherish the most."

Justin White, Minister / justinwhiteministries.com

"I want to MAX OUT being the best father and husband I can be. The PAY OUT is a loving family."

Stacy Meyer, Greensburg Boys Varsity Basketball Coach; 325 Career WINS

"I MAX OUT as a father by doing what my children want to do, even though it isn't my favorite thing to do, whether playing dolls or legos, or listening to them tell me something in a rambling manner, or doing something for the ninth time. The PAY OUT is that, 1) I know I've done my best 2) They get time with their dad."

Stacey Peters, Teacher/Coach

MOPO Memories

The Brew Crew traveled out West for this picture. We made a tour of the Rocky Mountains, Yellowstone National Park, Grand Tetons, Mount Rushmore, & The Badlands. Great memories with awesome scenery made for a Fun MOPO EXPERIENCE.

MOPO FAMILY

We are FAMILY. What a blessing to be a part of a family. God established the family when he created Adam and Eve. It's within a family where you learn how to relate to other people, how to support someone else, and how to be supported. Family is not easy. It is within a family that your biggest weaknesses are shown. Family can bring out the best in people and family can bring out the worst. As a father/mother, MOPO FAMILY is trying to give your best to your children. What does that mean? It means turning to God in prayer for your family daily. It means giving of your TIME and your ENERGY to LOVING UNCONDITIONALLY, being SUPPORTIVE, being FORGIVING, being COMMITTED and being ACCEPTING of your child. This takes work. It also takes others to help you be at your best: grandparents, aunts, uncles, neighbors, and friends. You have to be able to lean on these people as you navigate through raising your kids.

The MO (**MAX OUT**) in the MOPO (**MAX OUT PAY OUT**) Experience for HUSBAND and WIFE is…

- o   loving your spouse unconditionally daily
- o   pursuing your spouse daily
- o   putting your spouse's needs first daily & understanding you're on the same TEAM
- o   praying for your spouse daily
- o   being kind, spending time, & communicating with your spouse daily
- o   doing FUN things together

The PO (**P**AY **O**UT) in the MOPO (**M**AX **O**UT **P**AY **O**UT) Experience for HUSBAND & WIFE is:

- o   a lifelong marriage together, a bond that no man can separate.
- o   memories made over time.
- o   a lifetime friendship.
- o   blessings from the Lord as you are faithful to one another.
- o   growth in the fruits of the Spirit: love, joy, peace, patience, kindness, goodness, faith, gentleness, and self-control.

The MO (**M**AX **O**UT) in the MOPO (**M**AX **O**UT **P**AY **O**UT) Experience for MOM and DAD is…

- o   loving your child each day unconditionally.
- o   being consistent in your discipline of your child(ren).
- o   praying for your child daily and teaching the Bible to them.
- o   giving your time, energy, and attention to your child daily.
- o   providing your child with opportunities to grow.

The PO (**P**AY **O**UT) in the MOPO (**M**AX **O**UT **P**AY **O**UT) Experience for MOM and DAD is…

- o   a solid relationship formed with your kid(s).
- o   a respectful kid(s) with a love for life.
- o   seeds that have been planted for the Lord; hopefully, your kids will have a heart for God.
- o   life-lasting memories made.
- o   a legacy that can be passed down to your kids.
- o   growing in the fruits of the Spirit: love, joy, peace, patience, kindness, goodness, faith, gentleness, and self-control.

The MO (**M**AX **O**UT) in the MOPO (**M**AX **O**UT **P**AY **O**UT) Experience for CHILDREN is…

- o   loving, listening, and obeying your parents daily.
- o   playing, exploring, and using your imagination daily.

o   growing in the ways of the Lord daily (to know there is a Father in heaven who created them, who they can turn to, pray to, and know they are always loved).
o   finding something to be passionate about and investing time in it.

The PO (**PAY OUT**) in the MOPO (**MAX OUT PAY OUT**) Experience for CHILDREN is…

o   a respect for authority and a solid foundation in understanding unconditional love.
o   a heart for the Lord and the start of a relationship with God.
o   learning what their passions are in life.
o   having solid relationships that can be trusted.
o   growing in the fruits of the Spirit: love, joy, peace, patience, kindness, goodness, faith, gentleness, and self-control.

The MO (**MAX OUT**) in the MOPO (**MAX OUT PAY OUT**) Experience for GRANDPARENTS is…

o   loving your grandkids and kids unconditionally daily.
o   supporting your kids as they raise their family:
    •   a weekly phone call letting them know you are there for them
    •   a weekly text message telling them you are praying for them
    •   watching the grandkids to spend time with them and to give your kids a chance to be together
    •   taking your kids and their family out for dinner
    •   giving something small financially to help
    •   just spending time together.
    •   watching the grandkids to give mom and dad a break
    •   taking the grandkids out for ice cream, candy, or to pick out a toy from the store. Then, sending them back to Mom and Dad. ☺

The PO (**PAY OUT**) in the MOPO (**MAX OUT PAY OUT**) Experience for GRANDPARENTS is…

- o building solid relationships with their grandchildren.
- o growing closer in their relationship with their kids.
- o life-lasting memories made.
- o building a sound legacy that can be passed on from generation to generation.
- o growing in the fruits of the Spirit: love, joy, peace, patience, kindness, goodness, faith, gentleness, and self-control.

As you live out the MOPO FAMILY Experience, memories will be made. The days may feel like they go slowly, but the years will go quickly. MOPO FAMILY will ask:

What is something specific you want to work on to be a better MOPO (**M**AX **O**UT **P**AY **O**UT) husband/wife?

_____

_____

List 3 things that you would like to pray for your spouse:

1. _____

2. _____

3. _____

Write down your most memorable MOPO (**M**AX **O**UT **P**AY **O**UT) Experience you have had with your spouse:

_____

_____

Now, list a couple of MOPO (**M**AX **O**UT **P**AY **O**UT) Experiences you would like to plan for you and your spouse in the next month:

_____

_____

List the **P**AY **O**UT when you **M**AX **O**UT with your spouse:

_____

_____

What is something specific you want to work on to be a better MOPO (**M**AX **O**UT **P**AY **O**UT) Mom/Dad?

_____

_____

List 3 specific prayers you can pray over your family:

1. _____

2. _____

3. _____

Write down your most memorable MOPO (**M**AX **O**UT **P**AY **O**UT) Experience you have had as a family:

_____

_____

What is a MOPO (**M**AX **O**UT **P**AY **O**UT) Experience you can plan for your family to do in the up-coming month?

_____

_____

List the **P**AY **O**UT when you **M**AX **O**UT with your family:

_____

_____

What do you want your **P**AY **O**UT to be when you think about raising your family?

_____

_____

What is something specific you want to work on to be a better MOPO (**M**AX **O**UT **P**AY **O**UT) Grandparent?

_____

_____

List 3 specific prayers you can pray over your grand-kids:

1. _____

2. _____

3. _____

Write down your most memorable MOPO (**M**AX **O**UT **P**AY **O**UT) Experience with your grandkids:

_____

_____

What is a MOPO (**M**AX **O**UT **P**AY **O**UT) Experience you can plan with your grandkids in the next month?

_____

_____

List the **P**AY **O**UT when you spend time with your grand-kids:

_____

_____

MOPO LIFE: IT'S SHARING A HOTDOG AT THE BALLPARK WITH YOUR KID. MOPO THE DAY!

1 John 3:1

Look at how great a love the Father has given us, that we should be called God's children. And we are! The reason the world does not know us is that it didn't know Him.

MOPO LIFE: IT'S PLANTING A SEED AND WATCHING IT GROW. MOPO THE DAY!

Deuteronomy 6:4-9

"Listen, Israel: The Lord our God, the Lord is One. Love the Lord your God with all your heart, with all your soul, and with all your strength.

These words that I am giving you today are to be in your heart. Repeat them to your children. Talk about them when you sit in your house and when you walk along the road, when you lie down and when you get up. Bind them as a sign on your hand and let them be a symbol on your forehead. Write them on the doorposts of your house and on your gates."

MOPO LIFE: IT'S HANGING OUT WITH YOUR 5-MONTH OLD AT 2 IN THE MORNING. MOPO THE DAY!

Deuteronomy 5:16

Honor your father and your mother, as the Lord your God has commanded you, so that you may live long and so that you may prosper in the land the Lord your God is giving you.

MOPO LIFE: IT'S FISHING WITH YOUR 6-YEAR OLD. AFTER ONE CAST OF NOT CATCHING A FISH, HE SAYS, "DAD, I'M NOT A VERY GOOD FISHERMAN." YOU SAY, "PATIENCE, MY SON," A VIRTUE THAT CONTINUES TO CARRY ON TODAY. MOPO THE DAY!

Psalm 127:3-5

Sons are indeed a heritage from the Lord, children, a reward.

Like arrows in the hand of a warrior are the sons born in one's youth.

Happy is the man who has filled his quiver with them. Such men will never be put to shame when they speak with their enemies at the city gate.

MOPO LIFE: IT'S THE CHILD WHO WENT OUTSIDE AND PLAYED ALL DAY – PLAYED IN TREES, PLAYED IN WATER, PLAYED IN MUD, PLAYED WITH THE NEIGHBOR KIDS. THEN, HE FELL ASLEEP ON THE COUCH. MOPO THE DAY!

Proverbs 16:9

A man's heart plans his way,
But the Lord determines his steps.

MOPO LIFE: IT'S SITTING AROUND THE DINNER TABLE ENJOYING GOOD CONVERSATAION AND GREAT FOOD WITH YOUR FAMILY. THEN, YOU GET ICE CREAM FOR DESSERT. MOPO THE DAY!

Proverbs 31:10-12

Who can find a capable wife?
She is far more precious than jewels.
The heart of her husband trusts in her,
And he will not lack anything good.
She rewards him with good, not evil,
All the days of her life.

MOPO LIFE: IT'S WALKING HAND IN HAND 25 YEARS AFTER THE WEDDING. MOPO THE DAY!

Proverbs 5:18-19

Let your fountain be blessed,
And take pleasure in the wife of your youth.
A loving doe, a graceful fawn—
Let her breasts always satisfy you;
Be lost in her love forever.

MOPO LIFE: IT'S PICKING THE TOYS UP OFF THE FLOOR FOR THE 5TH TIME TODAY. MOPO THE DAY!

Proverbs 16:3

Commit your activities to the Lord
And your plans will be achieved.

MOPO LIFE: IT'S BEING PATIENT WITH YOUR MIDDLE SCHOOL DAUGHTER AND THEN BEING PATIENT SOME MORE. MOPO THE DAY!

Matthew 5:9

Blessed are the peacemakers,
because they will be called sons of God.

MOPO LIFE: IT'S GIVING YOUR KIDS A BEAR HUG AND KISS BEFORE GOING TO BED. MOPO THE DAY!

Luke 11:11-13

What father among you, if his son asks for a fish, will give him a snake instead of a fish? Or if he asks for an egg, will give him a scorpion? If you then, who are evil, know how to give good gifts to your children, how much more will the heavenly Father give the Holy Spirit to those who ask Him?"

MOPO LIFE: IT'S PLAYING DIFFERENT BOARD GAMES — *SORRY*, YAHTZEE, *CHUTES N LADDERS*, *NFL SHOWDOWN* — WITH YOUR 6-YEAR OLD UNTIL YOU WIN ONE. MOPO THE DAY!

John 20:4

The two (John & Peter) were running together, but the other disciple outran Peter and got to the tomb first. (John shows his competitiveness here☺)

MOPO LIFE: IT'S TAKING THE TIME TO PLAY WITH YOUR KIDS AFTER A HARD DAY AT WORK. MOPO THE DAY!

John 14:26

But the Counselor, the Holy Spirit—the Father will send Him in My name—will teach you all things and remind you of everything I have told you.

MOPO LIFE: IT'S SITTING AROUND THE CAMPFIRE MAKING SMORES WITH YOUR KIDS. MOPO THE DAY!

Psalm 139:13-16

For it was You who created my inward parts: You knit me together in my mother's womb.

I will praise You, because I have been remarkably & wonderfully made. Your works are wonderful, & I know this very well.

My bones were not hidden from You when I was made in secret, when I was formed in the depths of the earth.

Your eyes saw me when I was formless;

All my days were written in Your book & planned before a single one of them began.

MOPO LIFE: IT'S LETTING YOUR KID SET THE SLIP-N-SLIDE UP IN THE YARD. YOU KNOW THE GRASS WILL GET TORE UP, BUT OH THE MEMORIES YOUR KID WILL MAKE. MOPO THE DAY!

Romans 5:3

… but we also rejoice in our afflictions, because we know that affliction produces endurance, endurance produces proven character, and proven character produces hope.

MOPO LIFE: IT'S PASSING YOUR WISDOM DOWN TO THE NEXT GENERATION. MOPO THE DAY!

1 Corinthians 2:9

But as it is written: What no eye has seen and no ear has heard, and what has never come into a man's heart, is what God has prepared for those who love Him.

MOPO STORY

He was a 17-year-old junior in high school who had hopes of winning a Sectional in basketball. He had watched his older brother do it. All those early mornings of doing shooting workouts, playing AAU in the summer, and weight training after school had prepared him for this moment. He felt that it was his TEAM's time. He had put in the work. It was now time to step up to the challenge.

The PAY OUT: 32 minutes of battling for a lifetime of memories, a chance to cut down the nets, and a place in school history of winning the Sectional Championship.

MOPO THE DAY!

40

MOPO Wedding

One of the best days of my life when I married Elizabeth Ann Ahaus (July 6, 2002). We met at Marian College in the nursing program. I asked her to be my study partner in our Anatomy class. Here we are walking hand in hand after being pronounced husband & wife. Every day I get to hold her hand is a MOPO DAY!

TESTIMONIALS

"I have found in over 35 years of coaching that kids want two basic things: 1) Kids want someone to love & care about them 2) Kids want structure in their lives

I try to MAX OUT to our kids that we are a family – we pray together, love each other, & play together for each other.

I take deep pride in this fact, even today I get calls, texts, & cards from my kids. I always pray & hope that we've been able to help guide them in some small way in the right direction."

Dennis Bentzler, Taylor High School Boys Varsity Basketball Coach

"I would like my players/student-athletes to MAX OUT every day on controlling their attitude & effort. In doing so, they not only better themselves as an athlete/player, but more importantly as a person. Putting themselves in situations where they face struggle & adversity is the only way they will be able to grow & make the most of their situation & life. Going through life in cruise control will only lead to a life that is not MAXED OUT & not ever knowing how great they can possibly be."

Craig Ray, Strength & Conditioning Coach - Mooresville High School

"As a coach, I try to MAX OUT positive instruction, correcting athletes, & providing an enthusiastic environment for our players/TEAM to grow. The ultimate PAY OUT is having our TEAM play its best basketball possible at the end of the season."

Kip Staggs, Martinsville Boys Varsity Basketball Coach

"I have discovered that there is no replacement for time invested in a young man's life. Every young person needs someone other than a parent to be an advocate for them. And the best way you can be an advocate, is spending the time learning what to advocate for! So the PAY OUT is the players learn to trust . . . they learn to serve one another and how to genuinely care for others."

Casey Kolkman, Heritage Varsity Football Coach

"I want our players and coaching staff to MAX OUT always looking to improve in season and out. With the game constantly changing, it is important for us to keep up with those advancements so we can (PAY OUT) compete at a high level every year."

Mike Gillin, Mooresville High School Varsity Football Coach

"My PAY OUT is really based on relationships. We focus a lot with our coaching staff on building relationships with our girls. I challenge our staff to be able to know a couple things about each of our kids OTHER than basketball. It is really an eye-opening exercise to do."

Joe Smith, Speedway Girls Basketball Varsity Coach

"I tell my players all the time, the best part of coaching is when a former player comes back & you can tell it was a positive experience for him. I want my former players to take ownership in the program & want to follow the younger kids & know what they are going through."

Michael Wantz, Roncalli Boys Basketball Varsity Coach; 256 Career WINS

MOPO Sectional Champs

A truly rewarding experience to celebrate WINNING a Sectional Championship with my TEAMMATES. It was a true MOPO Experience. We had MAXED OUT by putting in the work, and our PAY OUT is a memory I will never forget. A MOPO CHAMPIONSHIP!

MOPO TEACHING/COACHING

Coach them up! There's a debate out there centered around the following question: *Have kids changed today from what they were 15-30-50 years ago?* Depending on who you talk to depends on the kind of answer you will get. I have been in education for almost 20 years now, and I can tell you this: Kids thrive when they know you care about them. Building relationships with your students/players should be at the foundation of your program. The challenge that presents itself is that not all kids will allow you to build that strong relationship. It takes effort and time. Many students and people in general have the what's-in-it-for-me attitude. As a teacher/coach, you have to learn the value of 'unconditional love.'

One of my favorite coaches to read about who showed unconditional love was John Wooden. The success he had with his UCLA teams was before my time, but the thing that intrigues me about Wooden is the way it seems he handled his players and the people with whom he came into contact. His coaching style was different in that he wasn't a screamer; he treated his players and students with respect. He still demanded a lot and expected a lot, but at the end of the day, his players respected him too. Here are some quotes from two of his players:

> "He wanted to win, but not more than anything . . . My relationship with him has been one of the most significant of my life . . . The consummate teacher, he taught us that the best you are capable of is victory enough, and that you can't walk until you crawl, that gentle but profound truth about growing up."

Kareem Abdul-Jabbar '69

"When I left UCLA in 1974 & became the highest paid player in the history of TEAM sports at that time, the quality of my life went down. That's how special it was to have played for John Wooden & UCLA."

Bill Walton '74

(http://www.motivational-story.com/John-Wooden.html)

Wooden had a vision with the way that he coached. Many of his quotes are still used today:

"Be more concerned with your character than your reputation, because your character is what you really are, while your reputation is merely what others think you are."

"If you are not making mistakes, then you're not doing anything. I'm positive a doer makes mistakes."

"Success comes from knowing that you did your best to become the best that you are capable of becoming."

John Wooden

It's this kind of vision and positive attitude that teachers/coaches today should be striving to have as we build relationships with our students/players to achieve the MOPO (**M**AX **O**UT **P**AY **O**UT) Experience. With the many different personalities that we deal with in the classroom on the playing field, it's critical that we can model what it means to be respectful and show love to our student-athletes.

How do we teach/coach and have this MOPO (**M**AX **O**UT **P**AY **O**UT) Experience? We must **M**AX **O**UT at being respectful, showing unconditional love, and being patient. It takes time to build relationships and trust with kids. This can make the job hard. But our **P**AY **O**UT is making a lasting impact on the students/players in which we come into contact each day. Sometimes, the **P**AY **O**UT is getting to WIN a championship with your players or seeing your student improve their test score from a C to an A. Often times, it isn't until down the road that we see our players/students go through a maturity that allows them to really understand the life lessons we were teaching them at the time we had them.

MOPO teaching/coaching is not for the faint of heart. It is for those individuals who have a real passion and desire to help the next generation succeed. **M**AX **O**UT your teaching/coaching so you can get a front row seat to watch the **P**AY **O**UT of your student/player getting his/her diploma and utilizing the life lessons you taught them in their adult lives.

The MO (**M**AX **O**UT) in the MOPO (**M**AX **O**UT **P**AY **O**UT) Experience for the TEACHER is…

- o always having your students' best interest in mind.
- o modeling unconditional love and grace with each one of your students.
- o being prepared every day with energy and enthusiasm – ready to execute a solid lesson plan.
- o staying up with the grading of the materials each week for your students.
- o being approachable for your students to ask questions to help them grow in class and in life.

The PO (**P**AY **O**UT) in the MOPO (**M**AX **O**UT **P**AY **O**UT) Experience for the TEACHER is…

- o seeing your students have success in the class.
- o building a trusting relationship with your students where they know you care.
- o ultimately helping your students pass your class so they can earn their diploma.
- o growing in the fruits of the Spirit: love, joy, peace, patience, kindness, goodness, faith, gentleness, and self-control.

The MO (**M**AX **O**UT) in the MOPO (**M**AX **O**UT **P**AY **O**UT) Experience for the COACH is…

o always having your players best interest in mind.
o modeling unconditional love and grace with your team daily.
o bringing a contagious enthusiasm and energy to practice each day.
o creating a plan covering the season that results in success for the team.
o always giving your best effort.

The PO (**P**AY **O**UT) in the MOPO (**M**AX **O**UT **P**AY **O**UT) Experience for the COACH is…

o TEAM success: winning games, winning conferences, winning championships.
o watching your players grow as players, in their sport, and as human beings.
o seeing your players graduate and move on to improve the world with lessons learned from you.
o building lifelong relationships where players will come back and support the program.
o growing in the fruits of the Spirit: love, joy, peace, patience, kindness, goodness, faith, gentleness, and self-control.

How will you **M**AX **O**UT your teaching/coaching today?

_____

_____

What do you hope the **P**AY **O**UT will be for you?

_____

_____

What will the **P**AY **O**UT be for your students/players?

_____

_____

What characteristics do you already have that make you a MOPO (**M**AX **O**UT **P**AY **O**UT) teacher/coach?

_____

_____

What MOPO (**M**AX **O**UT **P**AY **O**UT) characteristics do you want to improve on?

_____

_____

What are some ways you can improve the relationships you have with your class/team to make it a MOPO (**M**AX **O**UT **P**AY **O**UT) experience?

_____

_____

Think about one player or student who you have a difficult time relating to. Now, lift a prayer up to the Lord about helping this relationship to get better. Jot down one or two things you will do to help **M**AX **O**UT this relationship:

1. _____

2. _____

What are a few things this player/student could do to help **M**AX **O**UT the relationship?

_____

_____

What could the **P**AY **O**UT be if both parties are willing to do the things you listed to **M**AX **O**UT?

_____

_____

MOPO LIFE: IT'S THE TEACHER STAYING UP LATE GRADING PAPERS, FALLING ASLEEP AT THE TABLE, AND WAKING UP AT 4 AM TO FINISH GRADING. MOPO THE DAY!

Daniel 6:19-22

At the first light of dawn the king got up & hurried to the lions' den. When he reached the den, he cried out in anguish to Daniel. "Daniel, servant of the living God," the king said, "has your God whom you serve continually been able to rescue you from the lions?"

Then Daniel spoke with the king: "May the king live forever. My God sent His angel & shut the lions' mouths. They haven't hurt me, for I was found innocent before Him. Also, I have not committed a crime against my king."

MOPO LIFE: IT'S WHEN THE STUDENT SHOWS UP DAY AFTER DAY WITHOUT HIS HOMEWORK. THE TEACHER PATIENTLY SHOWS LOVE TO THE STUDENT. THE STUDENT BEGINS DOING HIS WORK. MOPO THE DAY!

Ephesians 2: 8-9

For by grace you are saved through faith, & this is not from yourselves; it is God's gift - - not from works, so that no one can boast.

MOPO LIFE: IT'S MAKING THE PRACTICE PLAN AND WATCHING YOUR TEAM GET BETTER. MOPO THE DAY!

2 Corinthians 12:9-10

But He said to me, "My grace is sufficient for you, for power is perfected in weakness." Therefore, I will most gladly boast all the more about my weaknesses, so that Christ's power may reside in me. So because of Christ, I am pleased in weaknesses, in insults, in catastrophes, in persecutions, and in pressures. For when I am weak, then I am strong.

MOPO LIFE: IT'S THE BONDS YOU FORM WITH YOUR PLAYERS & COACHES. MOPO THE DAY!

1 Corinthians 13:13

Now these three remain: faith, hope, and love. But the greatest of these is love.

MOPO LIFE: IT'S THE TEACHER STAYING LATE TO PREPARE FOR TOMORROW'S LESSON AND ARRIVING EARLY TO HELP MULTIPLE STUDENTS. REPEAT. MOPO THE DAY!

Matthew 28:18-20

Then Jesus came near & said to them, "All authority has been given to Me in heaven & on earth. Go, therefore, & make disciples of all nations, baptizing them in the name of the Father & of the Son & of the Holy Spirit, teaching them to observe everything I have commanded you. And remember, I am with you always, to the end of the age."

MOPO LIFE: IT'S WATCHING YOUR TEAM EXECUTE THE GAME PLAN. MOPO THE DAY!

Psalm 95:1-2

Come, let us shout joyfully to the Lord, shout triumphantly to the rock of our salvation!

Let us enter His presence with thanksgiving; let us shout triumphantly to Him in song.

MOPO LIFE: IT'S CELEBRATING IN THE LOCKER ROOM AFTER A BIG WIN. MOPO THE DAY!

Numbers 6:24-26

The Lord bless you and protect you;
The Lord make His face shine on you, and be gracious to you;
The Lord look with favor on you and give you peace.

MOPO LIFE: IT'S CALLING TIMEOUT —DOWN ONE WITH TEN SECONDS TO PLAY — DRAWING THE PLAY UP IN THE HUDDLE AND WATCHING THE KIDS EXECUTE IT FOR THE WIN. MOPO THE DAY!

Genesis 1:1

In the beginning, God created the heavens and the earth.

MOPO LIFE: IT'S WATCHING <u>ONE SHINING MOMENT</u> WITH YOUR TEAM. MOPO THE DAY!

1 Samuel 16:7

But the Lord said to Samuel, "Do not look at his appearance or his stature, because I have rejected him. Man does not see what the Lord sees, for man sees what is visible, but the Lord sees the heart.

MOPO LIFE: IT'S TALKING TO YOUR TEAM IN THE HUDDLE OR LOCKER ROOM, KNOWING EVERYONE IN THE HUDDLE IS ALL IN. MOPO THE DAY!

Hebrews 10:10

By this will, we have been sanctified through the offering of the body of Jesus Christ once and for all.

MOPO LIFE: IT'S STUDYING AND PREPARING SO THAT WHEN YOUR MOMENT COMES, YOU WILL BE READY. MOPO THE DAY!

John 15:7-8

Jesus said, "If you abide in Me, & My words abide in you, ask whatever you wish, and it will be done for you. My Father is glorified by this, that you bear much fruit, & so prove to be My disciples."

MOPO LIFE: IT'S KNOWING YOUR TEAM IS GETTING BETTER EVERY DAY. MOPO THE DAY!

1 Corinthians 15:22

For just as in Adam all die, so also in Christ all will be made alive.

MOPO LIFE: IT'S CUTTING DOWN THE NETS WITH YOUR TEAM AFTER WINNING THE CHAMPIONSHIP. MOPO THE DAY!

Luke 24:1-6

On the first day of the week, very early in the morning, they came to the tomb, bringing the spices they had prepared. They found the stone rolled away from the tomb. They went in but did not find the body of the Lord

Jesus. While they were perplexed about this, suddenly two men stood by them in dazzling clothes. So the women were terrified and bowed down to the ground. "Why are you looking for the living among the dead?" asked the men. "He is not here, but He has been resurrected!

MOPO LIFE: IT'S WATCHING YOUR SENIORS GRADUATE & MOVE ON WITH THE LIFE LESSONS YOU TAUGHT. MOPO THE DAY!

2 Peter 3:9

The Lord does not delay His promises, as some understand delay, but is patient with you, not wanting any to perish, but all to come to repentance.

MOPO STORY

He was a 17-year-old- kid, one of the younger students in his senior class. He found trouble with the law on a few occasions because of the crowd he had ran with and his many bad decisions. He had a God-given talent in the sport of basketball; there really wasn't anything he couldn't do on the court. Because of his low grades and many poor choices, there were no division one college coaches who would give him a chance. But then there was one. One coach who believed in second chances. One coach who believed in being patient. One coach who would give him that second chance.

After two years at a junior college, this young kid who had grown up was now making better decisions. He ended up playing for a major division one school and going to the NBA.

MOPO THE DAY!

TESTIMONIALS

"Players will learn the importance of how to control their attitude & effort in a positive way."

Mark James, Indiana Hall of Fame Boys High School Basketball Coach, Perry Meridian High School; 575 Career WINS; My High School Basketball Coach

"Players will have experience working toward a TEAM goal. They will learn how to handle winning/losing situations that will happen. We want players to do their best as an individual to become an important part of a TEAM concept."

John Holmes, Indiana Hall of Fame Boys High School Basketball Coach, Bloomington South High School; 836 Career WINS – currently most wins in Indiana High School Basketball Coaching History

"By being in the program, it will make the players become better leaders, teammates, and better people. The players will learn to sacrifice for the betterment of the group. Players will learn to have a genuine concern for their teammates & their coaches."

Andy Weaver, Plainfield Boys Varsity Basketball Coach; 314 Career WINS

"In our football program, we want to MAX OUT building relationships among our coaching staff & with our players. We love our players & want what we see is best for them."

Mark Bless, Avon High School Varsity Football Coach

"I want players to MAX OUT their ATTITUDE & EFFORT every day. Those are two things that they can control every day they get out of bed. I want their PAY OUT to be to ENJOY their LIFE. Life is too short."

Chad Ballenger, Hamilton Heights Boys Varsity Basketball Coach; 261 Career WINS

"As a Coach/Teacher/Parent, the greatest gifts you can provide a young person are life-lessons that enable them to be a productive & giving individual to their community. This community involves a future family, job, friends, as well as the town in which they live. Winners, in life, are individuals who have the ability to be their best at all times. It is my prayer that all of our former (& current) players have experienced enough lessons to always be at their best."

Bob Carter, Mooresville Boys Varsity Basketball Coach; 214 Career WINS

MOPO Coaching

Every year I look forward to attending the (Indiana High School Coaches Association) IBCA Clinic. I love seeing & talking to other coaches, listening to the coaches as they present, & trying to get a photo with the main coach who speaks. In this particular year, I was able to get a pic with Coach Matt Painter of Purdue. I have a great appreciation for the high level of coaching of Indiana High School Basketball Coaches, their time commitment, & their ability to get the most out of their players = MOPO COACHING!

MOPO SPORTS

Sports are fun! Growing up with an older brother and a dad who was a coach, I have always been into sports. I love watching them, playing them, and coaching them. Sports have always fed the competitive nature instilled in me. The goal was to try to win, but sports allowed for so many other life lessons to be learned:

o If you want to be good at something, you have to work at it.
o The best team on paper doesn't always win.
o In order to become a great team, you have to work well with others.
o You have to take responsibility for your play.
o You have to be disciplined both on and off the court.
o The best relationships are formed through trying to accomplish a unified goal.

Sports allowed for both the body and the mind to be stretched.

The MO (**M**AX **O**UT) in the MOPO (**M**AX **O**UT **P**AY **O**UT) Experience for PLAYERS is...

o to be coachable on a daily basis.
o to be a great teammate by encouraging others, supporting teammates, and putting others before yourself.
o to trust that your coaches have your best interest in mind.
o to know that getting better is a process; overnight success is a myth. You get better over time.
o working hard, competing hard, and giving your best effort each day.

The PO (**P**AY **O**UT) in the MOPO (**M**AX **O**UT **P**AY **O**UT) Experience for PLAYERS is…

- o team success: winning games, winning conference, and winning championships.
- o individual success and growing in your craft.
- o being able to compete at a high level.
- o forming lifelong friendships with your teammates and coaches.
- o knowing that if you can withstand the grueling sport season, you are ready for whatever life will throw at you.
- o graduating from your school with a diploma/degree.

MOPO (**M**AX **O**UT **P**AY **O**UT) Sport Questions to Answer:

What is your favorite MOPO sport?_____

As a coach, what are some things you can do better to **M**AX **O**UT (MO) your season?

_____

_____

As a player, what are some things you can do better to **M**AX **O**UT (MO) your season?

_____

_____

List 2 MOPO (**M**AX **O**UT **P**AY **O**UT) things you have learned from watching or playing sports?

1. _____
2. _____

List 3 things you want your induvial **P**AY **O**UT to be from the sport?

1. _____
2. _____
3. _____

List 3 things you want to be your **P**AY **O**UT for your team through the sport?

1. _____
2. _____
3. _____

MOPO LIFE: IT'S MAKING THE EXTRA EFFORT TO GAIN ANOTHER YARD. MOPO THE DAY!

Hebrews 12:1-2

Therefore since we also have such a large cloud of witnesses surrounding us, let us lay aside every weight & the sin that so easily ensnares us, & run with endurance the race that lies before us, keeping our eyes on Jesus.

MOPO LIFE: IT'S SHAKING HANDS – WIN OR LOSE – AFTER A HARD-FOUGHT GAME TO SHOW RESPECT FOR YOUR OPPONENT. MOPO THE DAY!

Psalm 23:1-4

The Lord is my shepherd; there is nothing I lack.
He lets me lie down in green pastures; He leads me besides quiet waters.
He renews my life; He leads me along the right paths for His name's sake.
Even when I go through the darkest valley, I fear no danger, for You are with me; Your rod & Your staff – they comfort me.

MOPO LIFE: IT'S STUDYING AND PREPARING FOR A TEST, A GAME, OR MATCH AND GOING OUT AND PERFORMING WITH YOUR BEST EFFORT. MOPO THE DAY!

2 Chronicles 20:20-21

In the morning they got up early & went out to the wilderness of Tekoa. As they were about to go out, Jehoshaphat stood and said, "Hear me, Judah & you inhabitants of Jerusalem. Believe in the Lord your God, & you will be established; believe in His prophets, & you will succeed." Then he consulted with the people & appointed some to sing for the Lord and some to praise the splendor of His holiness. When they went out in front of the armed forces, they kept singing:

Give thanks to the Lord, for His faithful love endures forever.

MOPO LIFE: IT'S STAYING UP LATE TO BE ENTERTAINED AND INSPIRED BY SPORTS: SUNDAY NIGHT FOOTBALL, MONDAY NIGHT FOOTBALL, THE WORLD SERIES GAMES, THURSDAY NIGHT FOOTBALL, FRIDAY NBA GAMES, SATURDAY COLLEGE FOOTBALL GAMES, AND SUNDAY REPEAT. MOPO THE DAY!

Ecclesiastes 2:24-25

There is nothing better for a man than to eat, drink, & to enjoy his work. I have seen that even this is from God's hand. For who can eat & who can enjoy life apart from Him?

MOPO LIFE: IT'S ALWAYS BEING READY. MOPO THE DAY!

Romans 8:31

What then are we to say about these things?

If God is for us, who is against us?

MOPO LIFE: IT'S GAME DAY. PLAY WITH HEART. PLAY WITH EMOTION. PLAY WIITH PASSION. PLAY FOR YOUR TEAMMATES. PLAY FOR YOUR SCHOOL. PLAY FOR YOUR COMMUNITY. LEAVE IT ALL ON THE COURT. MOPO THE DAY!

Isaiah 53:5-6

But He was pierced because of our transgressions,
Crushed because of our iniquities;
Punishment for our peace was on Him,
And we were healed by His wounds.
We all went astray like sheep;
We all have turned to our own way;
& the Lord has punished Him
For the iniquity of all.

MOPO LIFE: IT'S BASKETBALL: GET THE LOOSE BALL, MAKE CONTACT ON A SCREEN, TALK ON THE COURT, CHEER ON THE BENCH, AND BE A GREAT TEAMMATE. MOPO THE DAY!

2 Timothy 1:7

For God has not given us a spirit of fearfulness, but one of power, love, & sound judgment.

MOPO LIFE: IT'S FOOTBALL: HIT SOMEBODY, KNOW YOUR ASSIGNMENT, HUSTLE UNTIL THE WHISTLE, PLAY WITH ENTHUSIASM, AND BE A GREAT TEAMMATE. MOPO THE DAY!

2 Timothy 2:3

Share in the suffering as a good soldier of Christ Jesus.

MOPO LIFE: IT'S BASEBALL: HUSTLE, HIT, AND NEVER QUIT. MOPO THE DAY!

Galatians 5:22

But the fruit of the Spirit is love, joy, peace, patience, kindness, goodness, faith, gentleness, self-control. Against such things there is no law.

MOPO LIFE: IT'S HAVING YOUR FAVORITE SPORTING EVENT ON TV. TIME TO GET THE PIZZA, WINGS, POPCORN, NACHOS AND CHEESE, AND THE ICE CEREAM READY. MOPO THE DAY!

John 3:30

(Jesus) He must increase, but I must decrease.

MOPO LIFE: IT'S BASEBALL. THE COUNT IS 3-2 WITH THE BASES LOADED. TWO OUTS. BOTTOM OF THE NINTH. THE SCORE IS TIED 2-2. THE PITCHER WANTS THE BALL IN HIS HANDS. DO YOU WANT THE BALL? MOPO THE DAY!

Philippians 4:6

Don't worry about anything, but in everything, through prayer & petition with thanksgiving, let your requests be made known to God.

MOPO LIFE: IT'S GAMEDAY: IT'S BEING MENTALLY AND PHYSICALLY READY TO PLAY FOR ALL FOUR QUARTERS. MOPO THE DAY!

Deuteronomy 20:3-4

'Listen, Isreal: Today you are about to engage in battle with your enemies. Do not be fainthearted. Do not be afraid, alarmed, or terrified because of them. For the Lord your God is the One who goes with you to fight for you against your enemies to give you victory.'

MOPO LIFE: IT'S BASKETBALL. THE TEAM IS DOWN BY ONE POINT WITH EIGHT SECONDS TO PLAY IN THE GAME. THE SHOOTING GUARD DEMANDS THE BALL TO TAKE THE LAST SHOT. DO YOU WANT THE BALL IN YOUR HANDS? MOPO THE DAY!

Philippians 3:10-11

My goal is to know Him & the power of His resurrection & the fellowship of His sufferings, being conformed to His death, assuming that I will somehow reach the resurrection from among the dead.

MOPO LIFE: IT'S THE BEST PLAYER ON THE TEAM BEING THE LAST TO LEAVE THE GYM. SHE STAYED TO GET UP EXTRA SHOTS; BUT SHE ALSO STAYED TO PICK UP THE TRASH AND MAKE SURE THE LOCKER ROOM WAS CLEAN. #LEADBYEXAMPLE MOPO THE DAY!

1 Corinthians 11:1

Be imitators of me, as I also am of Christ.

MOPO LIFE: IT'S HITTING A HOLE IN ONE ON THE GOLF COURSE. MOPO THE DAY!

Colossians 3:14-15

Above all, put on love—the perfect bond of unity. And let the peace of the Messiah, to which you were also called in one body, control your hearts. Be thankful.

MOPO LIFE: SOCCER: IT'S KICKING A CORNER KICK IN THE GOAL. GOOOOOOOOOAAALLLLLLLL! MOPO THE DAY!

Luke 6:46-49

Jesus said, "Why do you call Me 'Lord, Lord,' & don't do the things I say? I will show you what someone is like who comes to Me, hears My words, & acts on them:

He is like a man building a house, who dug deep & laid the foundation on the rock. When the flood came, the river crashed against that house & couldn't shake it, because it was well built. But the one who hears & does not act is like a man who built a house on the ground without a foundation. The river crashed against it, & immediately it collapsed. And the destruction of that house was great!"

MOPO LIFE: IT'S CHEERING ON YOUR FAVORITE TEAM TO VICTORY. MOPO THE DAY!

Acts 9:15

But the Lord said to him, "Go! For this man (talking about Paul) is My chosen instrument to carry MY name before the Gentiles, kings, & the sons of Israel.

MOPO LIFE: IT'S CHEERING ON YOUR FAVORITE TEAM AFTER A LOSS. MOPO THE DAY!

Philemon 1:4-5

I always thank my God when I mention you in my prayers, because I hear of your love & faith towards the Lord Jesus & for all the saints.

MOPO LIFE IT'S GETTING UP EVERYDAY WITH AN ATTITUDE SAYING, "I'M GETTING BETTER TODAY!" MOPO THE DAY!

Acts 2:38

"Repent," Peter said to them, "and be baptized, each of you, in the name of Jesus the Messiah for the forgiveness of your sins, and you will receive the gift of the Holy Spirit."

MOPO LIFE: IT'S SUPER BOWL WEEKEND. STOCK UP ON PIZZA, CHICKEN WINGS, DONUTS, CHIPS AND SALSA, ICE CREAM, AND YOUR FAVORITE BEVERAGE. CHEER ON YOUR TEAM! MOPO THE DAY!

John 3:16-17

"For God loved the world in this way: He gave His One & Only Son, so that everyone who believes in Him will not perish but have eternal life. For God did not send His Son into the world that He might condemn the world, but that the world might be saved through Him."

MOPO STORY

She turned 40 and felt her body was falling apart. She had aches and pains in areas she hadn't felt before. She had gained a few pounds, and her friends encouraged her to run the half marathon with them. They began training together. It hurt in the beginning, but each week she found the motivation needed from her loving friends and started getting a little stronger – physically and mentally. She found herself craving exercise more and more. The pounds began to drop. Her aches and pains became more tolerable. She finished the 13.1 miles.

MOPO THE DAY!

TESTIMONIALS

"I want our players to MAX OUT their effort every day. We talk about 'Doing Today Well'. The result or PAY OUT of that will be an opportunity for them to be the best version of themselves."

Chris Holtmann, Ohio State Men's Basketball Coach

"Something I want our players to MAX OUT every day is to pursue excellence & to give their very best. In doing so, I want their PAY OUT to be them reaching their fullest potential. A verse that I think of referencing this is Galatians 6:9, "Let us not become weary in doing good, for at the proper time we will reap a harvest if we do not give up.""

Kyle Getter, Virginia Men's Assistant Basketball Coach

"How do I *MAX OUT* when I exercise," my simple response would have to simply be that I SHOW UP! I *MAX OUT* by choosing to make exercise apart of my daily life. I show up and move my body every day. I *MAX OUT* by taking advantage of being capable of doing something active every day. I am not the fastest, strongest, or most athletic individual in the room but I will always show up and give the best of my ability.

The daily dose of endorphins, sweat, cardiovascular health, feeling good, challenging myself, reaching goals, living an active life, fighting the tide of aging are huge *PAY OUTS* for maxing out with exercise. At the end of the day I *MAX OUT* because I want to feel good, look good and maintain a level of fitness that elongates my career as a firefighter and most importantly creates a foundation for aging gracefully with minimal physical deficits."

Brittany Craciunoiu, Firefighter; My Sister

MOPO EXERCISE

Be Active! You have set a goal to exercise throughout the year, but you find yourself struggling to stay motivated and find the time to get out and exercise. It's time to change your attitude. Time to MOPO (**M**AX **O**UT **P**AY **O**UT) Exercise. **M**AX **O**UT! Make a short-term goal and a long-term goal as to what you want to do. Then, attack your goals with the MOPO (**M**AX **O**UT **P**AY **O**UT) Attitude. For example, I set a goal for myself to run a mile every day for a year. I had to take one day at a time. I would set a goal to run one mile a day for a week and then do again the next week. I kept at it until I completed my goal. Each day I reminded myself of my MOPO Goal. Think about how you can **M**AX **O**UT to accomplish your goal, and then make a list of how it can **P**AY **O**UT for you. Understand that when you MOPO Exercise, it is a process. Take one day at a time, and MOPO the Day! It all starts with a healthy perspective in knowing when you **M**AX **O**UT your exercise, you will see a **P**AY **O**UT!

The MO (**M**AX **O**UT) in your MOPO (**M**AX **O**UT **P**AY **O**UT) Exercise Experience is...

- o   getting determined in your mind to want to exercise.
- o   praying to the Lord and getting mentally focused to exercise.
- o   setting a short and long-term exercise goal for yourself.
- o   doing the exercise throughout your week.
- o   staying motivated to complete your goals.

The PO (**P**AY **O**UT) in your MOPO (**M**AX **O**UT **P**AY **O**UT) Exercise Experience is...

o being more physically and mentally fit.
o losing weight.
o feeling better about yourself.
o growing in understanding yourself, your body, and becoming more at peace with yourself.

Write out your MOPO (**M**AX **O**UT **P**AY **O**UT) short-term exercise goal:

_____

_____

Write out your MOPO (**M**AX **O**UT **P**AY **O**UT) long-term exercise goal:

_____

_____

Write out how accomplishing your short-term goal(s) will PO (**P**AY **O**UT) for you:

_____

_____

Write out how accomplishing your long-term goal(s) will PO (**P**AY **O**UT) for you:

_____

_____

Getting yourself started in an EXERCISE plan is about being motivated and having an inner drive to want to do it. List 3 words that describe your MOPO Attitude as you begin your exercise program.

Word Examples: **Focused – Boom – Let's Go – Charged – Ready to Move**

_____

_____

MOPO LIFE: IT'S DOING ANOTHER REP. DOING ANOTHER SET. MOPO THE DAY!

Philippians 3:20-21

But our citizenship is in heaven, from which we also eagerly wait for a Savior, the Lord Jesus Christ. He will transform the body of our humble condition into the likeness of His glorious body, by the power that enables Him to subject everything to Himself.

MOPO LIFE: IT'S BEING HUMBLE, STAYING HUNGRY, AND BEING THANKFUL. MOPO THE DAY!

Proverbs 16:18

Pride comes before destruction,
And an arrogant spirit before a fall.

MOPO LIFE: IT'S WORKING HARD AND PLAYING HARD. MOPO THE DAY!

Psalm 3:3-4

But You, Lord, are a shield around me,
my glory, & the One who lifts up my head.
I cry aloud to the Lord,
and He answers me from His holy mountain.

MOPO LIFE: IT'S GIVING IT YOUR ALL – EVERY SINGLE DAY! MOPO THE DAY!

Colossians 3:12-15

Therefore, God's chosen ones, holy and loved, put on heartfelt compassion, kindness, humility, gentleness, and patience, accepting one another and forgiving one another if anyone has a complaint against another. Just as the Lord has forgiven you, so also you must forgive. Above all, put on love—the perfect bond of unity. And let the peace of the Messiah, to which you were also called in one body, control your hearts. Be thankful.

MOPO LIFE: IT'S MAKING IT FUN. MOPO THE DAY!

Zechariah 8:5

The streets of the city will be filled with boys and girls playing in them.

MOPO LIFE: IT'S DOING AN EXERCISE WORKOUT WITH YOUR DAUGHTER WHEN SHE SAYS, "DAD, YOU'RE REALLY STRONG," KNOWING THAT PHYSICALLY YOU ARE NOT THAT STRONG, BUT YOU ARE STRONG IN THE EYES OF THE ONE YOU WANT TO BE STRONG FOR. MOPO THE DAY!

Joel 1:3

Tell your children about it, and let your children tell their children, and their children the next generation.

MOPO LIFE: IT'S WHEN YOU DO THE LITTLE THINGS RIGHT THAT ALLOWS THE BIG THINGS TO HAPPEN. MOPO THE DAY!

Colossians 3:17

And whatever you do, in word and deed, do everything in the name of the Lord Jesus, giving thanks to God the Father through Him.

MOPO LIFE: IT'S WORKING HARD TO GET THE OPPORTUNITY TO HAVE SUCCESS. WORKING HARD DOESN'T GUARANTEE IT. MOPO THE DAY!

Psalm 27:3

Though an army deploy against me, my heart is not afraid;
Though war break out against me, still I am confident.

MOPO LIFE: IT'S GETTING UNCOMFORTABLE IN YOUR WORKOUT TO GO FURTHER; THE SAME IS TRUE IN LIFE. MOPO THE DAY!

Jeremiah 29:11-13

For I know the plans I have for you - - (this is) the Lord's declaration - - "plans for your welfare, not for disaster, to give you a future and a hope. You will call to Me & come and pray to Me, and I will listen to you. You will seek Me & find Me when you search for Me with all your heart.

MOPO LIFE: IT'S SETTING A GOAL AND WORKING TO ACHIEVE IT. MOPO THE DAY!

Daniel 6:10

When Daniel learned that the document had been signed, he went into his house. The windows in its upper room were opened toward Jerusalem, & three times a day he got down on his knees, prayed, & gave thanks to His God, just as he had done before.

MOPO LIFE: IT'S GETTING FOCUSED. SET THE TONE. MAKE SOMETHING HAPPEN. MOPO THE DAY!

Colossians 4:2

Devote yourselves to prayer; stay alert in it with thanksgiving.

MOPO LIFE: IT'S PUSHING YOURSELF TO THE NEXT LEVEL. MOPO THE DAY!

Philippians 4:13

I am able to do all things through Him who strengthens me.

MOPO LIFE: IT'S FINISHING –– FINISHING THE WORKOUT, THE GAME, THE CONVERSATION, THE JOB. MOPO THE DAY!

Philippians 3:7

But everything that was a gain to me, I have considered to be a loss because of Christ.

MOPO STORY

They had been married for three years and were ready to start a family. They spent time praying for a child. Three years later, they were still praying. It had brought friction and conflict to the marriage. They longed to have their own child and have a family of their own. They began to search other options. Both had agreed that they were open to adoption. As they began the process of adopting, the Lord answered their prayers with a little boy. As they went to meet the little boy, the wife began to feel very nauseous. She kept telling herself it was her nerves from becoming a new mom. As her nausea continued, she decided to take a pregnancy test. *Boom Baby!*

MOPO THE DAY!

TESTIMONIALS

"I want to MAX OUT the power of prayer. God has graciously given us His mighty power at our disposal. Prayer is how we tap into His power to do His will. When we MAX OUT by praying, God gives the PAY OUT in ways that are "immeasurably more than we ask or imagine, according to His power that is at work within us . . . "When we MAX OUT our prayers, God gives the PAY OUT for His glory."

Luke Proctor, Minister

"I want to do a better job of MAXING OUT a more prayerful life & spending more time praying for those specific individuals & events that are on my heart."

Brian Woodard, Plainfield Varsity Football Coach

"For me, it comes down to being more mindful of God throughout the entire day. I need to speak to God while I am going about my daily life. I need to talk with Him when I am challenged by a student situation . . . when I am blessed by a visit, call, or text from my children . . . when I am struggling through a tedious stack of papers or home project . . . when I am worried about finances or health . . . when I see His sun set or I hear the night sounds or I feel the breeze that He has sent across the earth that He has made. These are moments in my daily life in which I need to be speaking to my Creator. This is how I draw closer to God. This is how I MAX OUT my prayer life."

Brian Planker, Teacher/Coach

"I MAX OUT my day by trying to stay in constant prayer with God. I want my will to align with His will. The PAY OUT is knowing that no matter what circumstance is thrown at me during the day, I have confidence in knowing God will help me."

Beth Brewer, Nurse/My Beautiful Bride of 18 years

MOPO PRAYER

PRAY! Each of us is called to prayer. The Bible tells us that Jesus Christ spent many hours praying to the Father. As a Christian myself, prayer is something I continue to learn how to do. Thankfully, God only wants us to come before Him with an honest and open heart. We do not need to be eloquent in our speech, dress a certain way, or have a certain amount of money. God wants our time and attention. This takes practice. I have come a long way over the years in my prayer life, yet I still have a long way to go. Personally, I try to start each day in prayer, bringing my day to the Lord.

A sample morning prayer could sound like this:

Lord – God, my Father in Heaven, thank You for this new day. I lift up to you today my will. Help me to put others before myself, to be willing to serve, and to be willing to allow Your Spirit to work in me today. Let my thoughts be Your thoughts. Give me the tools and the wisdom to allow Your will to be done. Please have Your protective hand over my wife and kids. I yield today my work, my family, and my time to You that Your kingdom in Heaven may be felt here on this earth. Bless my friends and family. I ask these things in Jesus' name. AMEN.

Prayer can consist of many things. For example, prayer can include adoration – praising God for his greatness and admitting dependence on Him; confession – owning up to sin and asking for God's mercy and forgiveness; thanksgiving – thanking God for His many blessings; and petitions – asking God to move in the different areas of your life and for other people.

MOPO (**M**AX **O**UT **P**AY **O**UT) Prayer is knowing that you have the ability to pray at any time of the day or night to the Father who is sitting on the throne. **M**AXING **O**UT your prayer life is a maturity that a person comes to knowing that he/she can drop to their knees under any circumstance. The **P**AY **O**UT is knowing that you are handing your prayer request up to the One seated on the throne — the Maker of the universe, the One who has your best interest in mind, and the One who laid His life down for you.

The MO (**M**AX **O**UT) in your MOPO (**M**AX **O**UT **P**AY **O**UT) PRAYER Experience is…

- o taking time to surrender to God in Heaven.
- o having conversation with God anywhere at any time.
- o yielding the things of this life (family, job, marriage, bills, entertainment) to God.

The PO (**P**AY **O**UT) in your MOPO (**M**AX **O**UT **P**AY **O**UT) PRAYER Experience is…

- o handing over your thoughts/wants/needs/concerns to the Father who is sitting on the throne.
- o growing in your FAITH as you see God at work.
- o yielding control of your life to your Creator.
- o blessings that come from your Heavenly Father.

In the Bible, Colossians 4:2 says:

Paul writes, "Devote yourselves to prayer; stay alert in it with thanksgiving.

& Luke 5:30 states,

"But the Pharisees & their scribes were complaining to His disciples, "Why do you eat & drink with tax collectors and sinners?" Jesus replied to them, "The healthy don't need a doctor, but the sick do. I have not come to call the righteous, but sinners to repentance."

Write down 3 things you would like to MOPO (**M**AX **O**UT **P**AY **O**UT) Pray about:

1. _____
2. _____
3. _____

Take time to pray over those things right now.

What are the things that keep you from being a better prayer?

_____

_____

When you think of MOPO (**M**AX **O**UT **P**AY **O**UT) PRAYER, what can you do better to help **M**AX **O**UT your prayer life?

_____

_____

When you think of MOPO (**M**AX **O**UT **P**AY **O**UT) PRAYER, what would you like to see be your **P**AY **O**UT?

_____

_____

What are your strengths you have established in your prayer life to help you at MOPO PRAYER?

_____

_____

How and when will you MOPO PRAY moving forward?

_____

_____

MOPO LIFE: IT'S WHEN THE WORLD YOU ARE LIVING IN IS IN CHOAS. DROP TO YOUR KNEES AND PRAY. MOPO THE DAY!

1 Thessalonians 5:16-18

Rejoice always!
Pray constantly.
Give thanks in everything, for this is God's will for you in Christ Jesus.

MOPO LIFE: IT'S STARTING THE DAY ON YOUR KNEES IN PRAYER. MOPO THE DAY!

Luke 18:9-14

He also told this parable to some who trusted in themselves that they were righteous & looked down on everyone else: "Two men went up to the temple complex to pray, one a Pharisee and the other a tax collector. The Pharisee took his stand & was praying like this: 'God, I thank You that I'm not like other people –greedy, unrighteous, adulterers, or even like this tax collector. I fast twice a week; I give a tenth of everything I get.'

"But the tax collector, standing far off, would not even raise his eyes to heaven but kept striking his chest and saying, 'God, turn Your wrath from me - - a sinner!' I tell you, this one went down to his house justified rather than the other; because everyone who exalts himself will be humbled, but the one who humbles himself will be exalted."

MOPO LIFE: IT'S PRAYING WITH YOUR WIFE BEFORE GOING TO BED. MOPO THE DAY!

Matthew 6:6

But when you pray, go into your private room, shut your door, & pray to your Father who is in secret. And your Father who sees in secret will reward you.

MOPO LIFE: IT'S DRIVING IN THE CAR TALKING TO GOD. MOPO THE DAY!

Ephesians 6:18-19

With every prayer & request, pray at all times in the Spirit, & stay alert in this, with all perseverance & intercession for all the saints. Pray also for me (Paul), that the message may be given to me when I open my mouth to make known with boldness the mystery of the gospel.

MOPO LIFE: IT'S LISTENING TO YOUR 6-YEAR-OLD SAY THE DINNER PRAYER. MOPO THE DAY!

Colossians 4:2

Paul writes, "Devote yourselves to prayer; stay alert in it with thanksgiving.

MOPO LIFE: IT'S SAYING YOUR NIGHTLY PRAYER WITH YOUR FIVE-YEAR-OLD BEFORE TUCKING HIM INTO BED. MOPO THE DAY!

Matthew 6:9-13

Jesus said, "Therefore, you should pray like this:

Our Father in heaven, Your name be honored as holy. Your kingdom come. Your will be done on earth as it is in heaven. Give us today our daily bread.

And forgive us our debts, as we also have forgiven our debtors. And do not bring us into temptation, but deliver us from the evil one. For Yours is the kingdom & the power & the glory forever. AMEN.

MOPO LIFE: IT'S PRAYING OVER YOUR KIDDOS TO GO TO THE RIGHT COLLEGE, HAVE THE RIGHT JOB, AND MARRY THE RIGHT SPOUSE. MOPO THE DAY!

Mark 11:24

Jesus said, "Therefore, I tell you, all the things you pray & ask for---believe that you have received them, & you will have them.

MOPO LIFE: IT'S YIELDING CONTROL OF YOUR SINFUL NATURE BY GETTING ON YOUR KNEES. MOPO THE DAY!

Matthew 26:41

Jesus said, "Stay awake & pray, so that you won't enter into temptation. The spirit is willing, but the flesh is weak."

MOPO LIFE: IT'S LIFTING YOUR WORRIES TO GOD, KNOWING HE WILL TAKE CARE OF THEM. MOPO THE DAY!

Matthew 6:25-27

Jesus said, "This is why I tell you: Don't worry about your life, what you will eat or what you will drink; or about your body, what you will wear. Isn't life more than food & the body more than clothing? Look at the birds in the sky: they don't sow or reap or gather into barns, yet your heavenly Father feeds them. Aren't you worth more than they? Can any of you add a single cubit to his height by worrying?"

MOPO LIFE: IT'S SLOWING DOWN TO SAY A PRAYER FOR SOMEONE IN NEED. MOPO THE DAY!

Matthew 7:7-8

Jesus said, "Keep asking, & it will be given to you. Keep searching, & you will find. Keep knocking, & the door will be opened to you. For everyone who asks receives, & the one who searches finds, & to the one who knocks, the door will be opened.

MOPO LIFE: IT'S READING YOUR BIBLE AND APPLYING IT TO YOUR LIFE. MOPO THE DAY!

Luke 9:23-24

Then Jesus said to them all, "If anyone wants to come with Me, he must deny himself, take up his cross daily, and follow Me. For whoever wants to save his life will lose it, but whoever loses his life because of Me will save it."

MOPO STORY

They were a family of five. She was a stay at home mom; he worked long hours throughout the week. They had made a commitment to tithe 15% of his salary throughout the next year. There were weeks when the bills were stacked and they were unsure where the money would come from. She prayed while he worked. Many times the discussion came of taking their tithe money to pay the bills. She continued to pray. Each month a new blessing would be found; a $100 check from a loved one, a meal made by the neighbors, a tax return from the government.

God answering prayers.

MOPO THE DAY!

TESTIMONIALS

"I have a dream to MAX OUT my generosity to God. I have long wanted to give 25% of my income away to God & Christ honoring ministries around the world. My family & I have been working toward the goal for a while. However, as I get closer, I sense God asking me not to stop at 25%. How do I get to 30, 40, or even 50%? The PAY OUT would be exhilarating!"

Matt Nickoson, Minister

"I want to MAX OUT in helping others. I want to help my family, friends, players or students. The PAY OUT will be lifelong relationships."

David Benter, Brownstown Central Boys Varsity Basketball Coach; 378 Career WINS.

"I want to MAX OUT daily in loving Christ & loving those that cross in my path each day with all of my heart, soul, & mind. I want the PAY OUT to be in worshiping Christ & giving Him all the glory & honor as I point others to the Cross."

Matthew Hinds, Huntington North Girls Varsity Basketball Coach

"I believe, as a Christian, one of the ways I can MAX OUT & have the biggest impact in this life, is by how I manage my money. If I can be intentional with what God has blessed me with, this gives me an opportunity to be even more generous! Generosity allows lives to be changed by the love of the gospel and that is world-changing! My desire is to have as big of an impact as possible in my time on earth. The idea of "MAXING OUT" my finances (being as strategic as possible), in order to have the biggest "PAYOUT" (changing the world through generosity), is very inspiring to me and it drives me daily."

Cade Stockwell, Stewardship Minister

MOPO Friendships

Life is so much more enjoyable when you can experience it with friends. So thankful to have MOPO Friendships. We did a pedal wagon adventure in Cincinnati. Good memories as we celebrated my wife's 40th Birthday. MOPO the Day!

MOPO SERVE

People Matter. Do you live your life in such a way that the people around you know that they matter? Do you take time to listen? To learn a person's name? To learn a person's story? How often do you put the needs of others before your own? *Jesus did*. He took time to listen to the woman at the well. He took time to heal the sick. He took time to feed the hungry. Jesus showed His ultimate love for us by sacrificing Himself on the cross. He died for you. <u>You matter to Him!</u>

We live in a society that looks out for number one, a society where people think about themselves before thinking of others. I grew up loving the game of basketball. I was very fortunate to be able to play basketball in high school and college and be part of a lot of good teams. I loved playing on a team where guys were unselfish, cared about each other, and wanted to win more than be acknowledged for individual honors. When I wake up each morning, I try to keep two things in perspective: be humble and be thankful.

In order to stay humble and be thankful, one must be willing to SERVE. One must live in a way that shows the people around them that they matter. MOPO SERVE means to sacrifice — to give up your own time and efforts to help another person out. The challenge is to think of ways you can INVEST and SERVE others and then go do it. MOPO SERVE!

Here is a list of things you could do:

o   Check in on a neighbor: mow their grass, take them a meal, or buy them a gift card.

o   Write a letter to a prisoner.
o   Call to check in on a relative: a grandparent, an aunt/uncle, or a cousin.
o   Text a friend telling them you are praying for them.
o   Give blood.
o   Go visit someone in the hospital.
o   Sponsor a kid going to CIY, FCA, or a church camp over the summer.
o   Check in on a widow.

The MO (**M**AX **O**UT) in the MOPO (**M**AX **O**UT **P**AY **O**UT) SERVE Experience is...

o   being able to put others before yourself; live by the JOY acronym: **J**ESUS – **O**THERS – **Y**OURSELF.
o   being intentional about how you use your time.
o   looking for opportunities to pour into others.
o   being an encourager, showing love to all (even your enemies), and being a friend.

The PO (**P**AY **O**UT) in the MOPO (**M**AX **O**UT **P**AY **O**UT) SERVE Experience is...

o   growing in relationship with other people.
o   feeling good knowing you have helped another person.
o   growing in the Lord as you look more like Jesus.
o   the person you are serving will be blessed.

What attributes do you have that will help you in MOPO (**M**AX **O**UT **P**AY **O**UT) SERVING others?

_____

_____

Think about ways in your life where you demonstrate living out that people matter. How do you specifically live that out? & What is something you could change to put your focus on others?

_____

_____

In serving others, what do your children or students see that they could model?

_____

_____

In the past, what has kept you from MOPO (**M**AX **O**UT **P**AY **O**UT) SERVING others?

_____

_____

Make a specific list of how you can MOPO (**M**AX **O**UT **P**AY **O**UT) SERVE this week. Then, go do it!

_____

_____

_____

After you MOPO (**M**AX **O**UT **P**AY **O**UT) SERVE, how will this **P**AY **O**UT for you?

_____

_____

After you MOPO (**M**AX **O**UT **P**AY **O**UT) SERVE, how will this **P**AY **O**UT for the ones you are serving?

_____

_____

MOPO LIFE: IT'S MOVING DAY FOR YOUR NEIGHBOR, AND THE FORECAST SHOWS RAIN ALL DAY. YOU HAD PLANNED TO WATCH THE FOOTBALL GAME ON TV, BUT YOU DECIDE TO GO GET WET HELPING YOUR NEIGHBOR MOVE INSTEAD. MOPO THE DAY!

Psalm 149: 4

For the Lord takes pleasure in His people;
He adorns the humble with salvation.

MOPO LIFE: IT'S STEPPING UP TO DO THE DISHES FOR YOUR WIFE WHOSE HAD A LONG DAY WITH THE KIDS. MOPO THE DAY!

Colossians 3:18-21

Wives, be submissive to your husbands, as is fitting in the Lord.
Husbands, love your wives and don't become bitter against them.
Children, obey your parents in everything, for this is pleasing in the Lord.
Fathers, do not exasperate your children, so they won't become discouraged.

MOPO LIFE: IT'S HAVING AN IMPACT. OUR IMPACT WILL NOT BE MEASURED BY THE AMOUNT OF MONEY WE MADE OR THE JOB WE HAD BUT ON THE RELATIONSHIPS WE FORMED. MOPO THE DAY!

Luke 5:30

"But the Pharisees & their scribes were complaining to His disciples, "Why do you eat & drink with tax collectors and sinners?" Jesus replied to them, "The healthy don't need a doctor, but the sick do. I have not come to call the righteous, but sinners to repentance."

MOPO LIFE: IT'S INVESTING IN OTHERS: YOUR TIME, YOUR MONEY, AND YOUR ENERGY. MAKE A DIFFERENCE IN SOMEONE ELSE'S LIFE. MOPO THE DAY!

Proverbs 19:17

Kindness to the poor is a loan to the Lord,
And He will give a reward to the lender.

MOPO LIFE: IT'S INVESTING IN OTHERS AND HAVING YOUR PERSPECTIVE CHANGED. MOPO THE DAY!

Mark 10:43-45

Jesus said, "But it must not be like that among you. On the contrary, whoever wants to become great among you must be your servant, and whoever wants to be first among you must be a slave to all. For even the Son of Man did not come to be served, but to serve, & to give His life—a ransom for many."

MOPO LIFE: IT'S WHEN THE MASTER WASHED THE FEET OF HIS DISCIPLES. WHOOSE FEET HAVE YOU WASHED TODAY? MOPO THE DAY!

John 13:12-15

When Jesus had washed their feet and put on His robe, He reclined again and said to them, "Do you know what I have done for you? You call Me Teacher and Lord. This is well said, for I am. So if I, your Lord and Teacher, have washed your feet, you also ought to wash one another's feet. For I have given you an example that you also should do just as I have done for you."

MOPO LIFE: IT'S GIVING FINACIALLY TO A MISSIONARY. MOPO THE DAY!

Mark 16:15

Then He said to them, "Go into all the world and preach the gospel to the whole creation."

MOPO LIFE: IT'S TAKING TIME TO SHOP WITH YOUR TEENAGED DAUGHTER. MOPO THE DAY!

1 Timothy 4:12

No one should despise your youth; instead, you should be an example to the believers in speech, in conduct, in love, in faith, in purity.

MOPO LIFE: IT'S MOWING THE NEIGHBORS YARD WHILE HE RECOVERS FROM SURGERY. MOPO THE DAY!

Matthew 10:42

Jesus said, "And whoever gives just a cup of cold water to one of these little ones because he is a disciple - - I assure you: He will never lose his reward!"

MOPO LIFE: IT'S MAKING A MEAL FOR THE COUPLE WITH A NEW BABY. MOPO THE DAY!

Mark 9:35

Sitting down, He called the Twelve & said to them, "If anyone wants to be first, he must be last of all and servant of all."

MOPO LIFE: IT'S CHECKING ON YOUR NEIGHBOR WHO JUST LOST HER HUSBAND. MOPO THE DAY!

Matthew 25:34-40

Then the King will say to those on His right, 'Come, you who are blessed by My father, inherit the kingdom prepared for you from the foundation of the world.

For I was hungry & you gave Me something to eat;
I was thirsty & you gave Me something to drink;
I was a stranger & you took Me in;
I was naked & you clothed Me;
I was sick & you took care of Me;
I was in prison & you visited Me.'

"Then the righteous will answer Him, 'Lord, when did we see You hungry & feed You, or thirsty and give You something to drink? When did we see You a stranger & take You in, or without clothes & clothe You? When did we see You sick, or in prison, & visit You?'

"And the King will answer them, 'I assure you: Whatever you did for one of the least of these brothers of Mine, you did for Me.'

MOPO LIFE: IT'S USING YOUR GOD-GIVEN ABILITIES TO HELP BRING HIS KINGDOM TO THIS EARTH. MOPO THE DAY!

1 Peter 4:10-11

Based on the gift they have received, everyone should use it to serve others, as good managers of the varied grace of God.

MOPO LIFE: IT'S GIVING YOUR ELDERLY GRANDPARENTS A PHONE CALL TO CHECK IN ON THEM. MOPO THE DAY!

Galatians 6:9

So we must not get tired of doing good, for we will reap at the proper time if we don't give up.

MOPO LIFE: IT'S TELLING YOUR SIBLING YOU LOVE THEM. MOPO THE DAY!

Philippians 2:3

Do nothing out of rivalry or conceit, but in humility consider others as more important than yourselves.

MOPO LIFE: IT'S STEPPING UP TO CLEAN THE TOILETS. MOPO THE DAY!

Matthew 26:42

Again, a second time, He (Jesus) went away & prayed, "My Father, if this cannot pass unless I drink it, Your will be done."

MOPO LIFE: IT'S GIVING BLOOD. MOPO THE DAY!

Luke 22:19-20

And Jesus took bread, gave thanks, broke it, gave it to them, and said, "This is My body, which is given for you. Do this in remembrance of Me."

In the same way He also took the cup after supper and said, "This cup is the new covenant established by My blood; it is shed for you."

MOPO STORY

He had a dream: to own a boat. He had put himself through college and now had a good paying job. He worked and saved, worked and saved, and worked and saved. After five years, he had enough to buy the boat of his dreams and made the purchase. It was on one of his boat adventures that he met his future wife. He invited friends to take part and made many fun life memories. The couple raised a family and now the boat is used to give his grandkids life experiences.

MOPO THE DAY!

TESTIMONIALS

"I have been blessed with fulfilling a dream of owning a house boat where we have spent time with friends & family swimming, eating, talking, playing games, & focusing on our time together away from our normal hectic daily routine. The PAY OUT is building relationships with family, friends, & God. Memories, stories, values, & more of God's wonders are experienced at the boat."

Rick Brewer, Retired Educator/Middle School AD/ My Dad

"Vacations are special because you get to break away from life's stress & responsibility to spend time with people that you love. My wife & I try to MAX OUT these times by planning special events, being spontaneous, & saying "YES" more often to our children's requests. The PAY OUT is life long family memories!"

Jason Uhlrich, Administrator

MOPO Vacation

Lots of memories made when our crew stayed in a cabin in Michigan with my wife's side of the family as we celebrated 50 years of marriage for Ted & Vicki Ahaus. WOW! Thankful for their example of a MOPO Marriage and time spent together. MOPO the Day!

MOPO VACATION

Time for FUN! VACATION: a time to get away from work and the stresses of life — to go do something FUN, see something breathtaking, to take a break from your everyday schedule. MOPO (**M**AX **O**UT **P**AY **O**UT) VACATION is getting the most out of your trip. **M**AXING **O**UT: the sun on the beach, the swim in the ocean, the hike in the mountains, the food on the cruise ship, the extra sleep in the hotel room. What's the **P**AY **O**UT? Getting away from your everyday routine, spending time with your significant other and family, and/or seeing parts of the country/world you have never seen.

What is your favorite vacation destination? Going to the beaches of Florida? Getting on a cruise ship to go to the Bahamas? Hiking the mountains of Colorado? Flying to Paris? Whatever your favorite spot, being able to **M**AX **O**UT your vacation experience is a must. You have worked hard all year, and having an opportunity to go do the experience is a **P**AY **O**UT in and of itself.

The MO (**M**AX **O**UT) in the MOPO (**M**AX **O**UT **P**AY **O**UT) VACATION Experience is...

- o working and saving up enough money to go on the vacation.
- o packing and getting to your destination.
- o enjoying each day by doing the things you don't normally get to do at home.
- o sharing the experience with your loved ones.

The PO (**PAY OUT**) in the MOPO (**M**AX **OUT PAY OUT**) VACATION Experience is...

o making new memories.
o having new life experiences.
o getting a break from work and everyday life stresses.

Make a list of the MOPO VACATION destinations you would like to visit.

_____

_____

_____

Now write down one MOPO VACATION destination you want to visit this year.

_____

_____

Write down one thing you want to do to **M**AX **O**UT your MOPO VACATION experience.

_____

_____

What do you hope will be the **P**AY **O**UT of your MOPO VACATION experience?

_____

_____

MOPO LIFE: IT'S GOING FOR DONUTS AND ICE-CREAM. MOPO THE DAY!

Romans 8:1

Therefore, no condemnation now exists for those in Christ Jesus.

MOPO LIFE: IT'S A DISNEY TRIP OVER FALL BREAK – 4 KIDS, 4 HOURS OF SLEEP, ALL DECKED OUT IN MICKEY MOUSE GEAR, ON A MISSION TO CLOSE DOWN THE PARK. MOPO THE DAY!

Romans 8:28

We know all things work together for the good of those who love God: those who are called according to His purpose.

MOPO LIFE: IT'S HOPPING ON A PLANE TO GO TO THE BEACH FOR THE WEEKEND SO YOU CAN FEEL THE SAND BETWEEN YOUR TOES. MOPO THE DAY!

Colossians 1:16

Because by Him everything was created, in heaven & on earth, the visible & the invisible, weather thrones or dominions or rulers or authorities—

All things have been created through Him & for Him.

MOPO LIFE: IT'S STOPPING AT THE GAS STATION TO PICK OUT YOUR FAVORITE SNACK. MOPO THE DAY!

Exodus 31:18

When He finished speaking with Moses on Mount Sinai, He gave him the two tablets of the testimony, stone tablets inscribed by the fingers of God.

MOPO LIFE: IT'S HAVING THE CHOICE BETWEEN ICE CREAM WITH SPRINKLES OR WITHOUT. ALWAYS TAKE THE SPRINKLES. MOPO THE DAY!

Colossians 3:23-24

Whatever you do, do it enthusiastically, as something done for the Lord and not for men, knowing that you will receive the reward of an inheritance from the Lord—you serve the Lord Christ.

MOPO LIFE: IT'S WHEN YOUR NUMBER HITS ON THE ROULETTE WHEEL. MOPO THE DAY!

Proverbs 11:24

One person gives freely, yet gains more;
Another withholds what is right, only to become poor.

MOPO LIFE: IT'S HIKING TO THE WATERFALL. SO BEAUTIFUL! MOPO THE DAY!

Psalm 91:1-2

The one who lives under the protection of the Most High dwells in the shadow of the Almighty. I will say to the Lord, "My refuge & my fortress, my God, in whom I trust."

MOPO LIFE: IT'S HANGING OUT ON A BOAT WITH A DRINK IN YOUR HAND AND THE SUN'S RAYS HITTING YOUR BACK. MOPO THE DAY!

Psalm 25:4-5

Make Your ways known to me, Lord;

Teach me Your paths.
Guide me in Your truth & teach me, for You are the God of my salvation;
I wait for You all day long.

MOPO LIFE: IT'S GETTING UP EARLY TO WATCH THE SUNRISE. MOPO THE DAY!

Lamentations 3:22-23

Because of the Lord's faithful love we do not perish,
For His mercies never end.
They are new every morning; great is Your faithfulness!

MOPO LIFE: IT'S COLLECTING SEA SHELLS WHILE WALKING ON THE BEACH. MOPO THE DAY!

Galatians 2:19-20

For through the law I have died to the law, that I might live to God. I have been crucified with Christ; and I no longer live, but Christ lives in me. The life I now live in the flesh, I live by faith in the Son of God, who loved me and gave Himself for me.

MOPO LIFE: IT'S LETTING YOUR TEN-YEAR OLD BURY YOU IN THE SAND. MOPO THE DAY!

John 3:30

He (Jesus) must increase, but I must decrease.

MOPO LIFE: IT'S EXPIERENCING THE SNOW AT THE TOP OF THE MOUNTAIN IN THE MIDDLE OF JULY. MOPO THE DAY!

John 3:13-14

Jesus said, "Everyone who drinks from this water will get thirsty again. But whoever drinks from the water that I give him will never thirst again—ever! In fact, the water I will give him will become a well of water springing up within him for eternal life."

MOPO LIFE: IT'S DRIVING ACROSS THE COUNTRY TO SEE THE GRAND CANYON. MOPO THE DAY!

Romans 13:9

The commandments:
Do not commit adultery,
Do not murder,
Do not steal,
Do not covet,

And if there is any other commandment—all are summed up by this: You shall love your neighbor as yourself.

MOPO LIFE: IT'S GOING TO A DIFFERENT COUNTRY TO EXPERIENCE A NEW CULTURE. MOPO THE DAY!

Matthew 6:33

"But seek first the kingdom of God and His righteousness & all these things will be provided for you."

MOPO LIFE: IT'S DRIVING THROUGH THE NIGHT TO REACH THE OCEAN. MOPO THE DAY!

Romans 8:38-39

For I am persuaded that neither death nor life, nor angels nor rulers,

Nor things present, nor things to come, nor powers, nor height, nor depth, nor any other created thing will have the power to separate us from the love of God that is in Christ Jesus our Lord!

MOPO LIFE: IT'S DEEP SEA FISHING IN THE ATLANTIC OCEAN. MOPO THE DAY!

John 21:5-6

"Men," Jesus called to them, "you don't have any fish, do you?"

"No," they answered.

"Cast the net on the right side of the boat," He told them, "and you'll find some." So they did, and they were unable to haul it in because of the large number of fish.

MOPO LIFE: IT'S WALKING THE FREEDOM TRAIL IN BOSTON. MOPO THE DAY!

John 10:27-28

Jesus said, "My sheep hear My voice, I know them, and they follow Me. I give them eternal life, and they will never perish—ever! No one will snatch them out of My hand."

MOPO LIFE: IT'S SEEING THE WILDLIFE IN YELLOWSTONE WALK UP TO YOUR CAR. MOPO THE DAY!

Isaiah 40:28-31

Do you not know?
Have you not heard?
Yahweh is the everlasting God, the Creator of the whole earth.
He never grows faint or weary;
There is no limit to His understanding.
He gives strength to the weary and strengthens the powerless.
Youths may faint and grow weary, and young men stumble & fall,
But those who trust in the Lord will renew their strength;
They will soar on wings like eagles;
They will run and not grow weary;
They will walk and not grow faint.

MOPO LIFE: IT'S SINGING THE NATIONAL ANTHEM AT THE STEPS OF MOUNT RUSHMORE. MOPO THE DAY!

Romans 12:1

Therefore, brothers, by the mercies of God, I urge you to present your bodies as a living sacrifice, holy and pleasing to God; this is your spiritual worship.

MOPO LIFE: IT'S WATCHING TWO MOVIES YOU HAVE NEVER SEEN ON THE PLANE RIDE. MOPO THE DAY!

Proverbs 12:25

Anxiety in a man's heart weights it down, but a good word cheers it up.

MOPO LIFE: IT'S BEING FIRST IN LINE FOR YOUR FAVORITE ROLLERCOASTER. MOPO THE DAY!

Proverbs 19:23

The fear of the Lord leads to life;
One will sleep at night without danger.

MOPO LIFE: IT'S SITTING ON THE HOUSE BOAT, PLAYING CARDS, AND LISTENING TO YOUR FAVORITE MUSIC. MOPO THE DAY!

Romans 12:13

Share with the saints in their needs; pursue hospitality.

MOPO STORY

They were a family of four from Indiana. She was a school teacher and he was a business man. They had saved up, planned, and were taking a family trip for two weeks out West to see the Grand Canyon, Mt Rushmore, & Yellowstone National Park. As they approached their camp site to set up the tent, a huge bison strutted through the park. The family was in awe of its size. The trip consisted of many hikes surrounded by lots of wildlife, waterfalls, and breathtaking scenery created by God. The addition of nightly campfires with the making of smores made for a successful trip. Lots of memories made.

MOPO THE DAY!

TESTIMONIALS

"I *MAX OUT* by being excited about watching my favorite movie. The *PAY OUT* for me is the satisfaction I get from doing something I enjoy."

Heather Brewer, Paralegal/Sister-in-law

"I *MAX OUT* my movie experience by eating as much popcorn and drinking as much diet mountain dew as I can. The *PAY OUT* for me is saying that I have seen the latest movie that Hollywood has to offer."

Scott Kenworthy, Manager

MOPO MOVIES

LIGHTS—CAMERA—ACTION! Sitting down to watch a good movie can allow us to take a break from the everyday stresses of life. Those movies characterized by action, drama, horror, or comedy can help feed on our emotions. Every movie that is made hopes the audience will have a MOPO (**M**AX **O**UT **P**AY **O**UT) Experience. In order to have that experience, many people want to watch a movie with popcorn. What do you put on your popcorn? Butter? Cheese? Salt? Do you like it plain? One of the things Jesus calls us to do is be the salt of the earth. In the Bible, Matthew 5:13, Jesus says: "You are the salt of the earth." What does that mean? It means as a disciple of Christ, we are to flavor the world around us with God's love and direction. We are to preserve the things that are of value in this life from the sin and hate that can be so rampant in our world. This is a heavy responsibility.

The world needs more salt in it. <u>What are you doing today to be the salt</u>?

Whatever you are – a teacher/coach, a husband/wife, a father/mother, a son/daughter, an employee, a neighbor – we are all given an opportunity to be salt on a daily basis. What does that look like?

Teacher/Coach – It's making time for your students/athletes. It's building a trust with your players. It's modeling strong character and showing unconditional love.

Husband/Wife – It's being committed to one person – caring and loving your life-long partner each day and putting their needs before your own. It's loving your spouse unconditionally.

Father/Mother – It's loving your kids unconditionally every day. It's being willing to discipline and show tough love. It's making time to play and hang out with your kids. It's making a phone call to see how your kids are doing.

Son/Daughter – It's loving your parents unconditionally. It's listening, trusting, and obeying your parents. It's taking time to check in on your parents to see how they are doing.

Employee – It's showing up every day ready to work. It's trusting and obeying your boss. It's speaking positive about your co-workers/boss and being thankful for your job.

Neighbor – It's taking time to check in on your neighbor, being there when and if your neighbor ever needs you: to mow their grass, take them a meal, collect their mail, take their trash out, or be a listening ear.

The MO (**M**AX **O**UT) in being SALT in a fallen world is…

- o   being an ambassador for Christ.
- o   being the light & peace in an uncomfortable situation.
- o   sharing the love of Christ.

The PO (**P**AY **O**UT) in being SALT in a fallen world is…

- o   growing in your walk with Christ.
- o   spreading love to your neighbor.
- o   growing in relationship with the people in your world.

The MO (**M**AX **O**UT) in the MOVIE Experience is…

- o   sitting in heated seats that lay back.
- o   having buttered popcorn with SALT.
- o   watching the movie on the big screen with surround sound.

The PO (**P**AY **O**UT) in the MOVIE Experience is...

- o   having your emotions stirred.
- o   learning something new from the movie.
- o   watching the movie with friends and loved ones.
- o   getting to eat popcorn, candy, and drink pop. ☺

There are many movies out there that could represent the MOPO (**M**AX **O**UT **P**AY **O**UT) way of LIFE. I have chosen 6 of my favorites:

OPEN RANGE (Rated R): Starring Kevin Costner and Robert Duvall, this western thriller allows you to see how Duvall mentors and leads Costner throughout the movie. One of the scenes that sticks out to me is when Duvall and Costner are in the local store before they are going to battle for their lives. Duvall buys two candy bars from the storeowner who speaks very highly of the candy, but we learn the storeowner has never actually tried the candy because it's too expensive. Duvall comments to the store owner, "You have had this candy all along and have never tried it?"

MOPO LIFE: TAKE TIME TO ENJOY THE GOOD THINGS IN LIFE.

SHAWSHANK REDEMPTION (Rated R): Starring Tim Robbins and Morgan Freeman, this drama takes the viewer into the depths of a high security prison. The movie allows you to see the relationships formed in a prison and how Robbins is able to bring dignity and respect back to some of the inmates by taking the time to share his talents in getting a library and helping the guards with their taxes.

MOPO LIFE: USE YOUR TALENTS TO HELP OTHERS.

BIG (Rated PG): Starring Tom Hanks, this comedy-drama is about a 13-year-old boy who wishes to be BIG and has his wish come true. As he gets thrown into an adult world, he still has the charisma of a young boy who never loses his childlike innocence. In one scene, he gets his first paycheck and screams out, "$187!" He has never had so much money. His co-workers think they aren't getting paid enough. I love his attitude and innocence in this scene.

MOPO LIFE: BE THANKFUL AND APPRECIATE YOUR BLESSINGS.

PASSION OF THE CHRIST (Rated R): Starring Jim Caviezel and written by Mel Gibson, this powerful drama covers the last 12 hours of Jesus's life. In this extremely violent movie, we see how Jesus sacrificed himself for the love of us. It really makes you have a better understanding of what Jesus went through to save us from our debt of sin.

MOPO LIFE: BE HUMBLE AND LIVE FOR CHRIST.

HOOSIERS (Rated PG): Starring Gene Hackman and Dennis Hopper, this Sports Drama covers the David vs Goliath story of Hoosier Basketball when little Milan beat Muncie Central in the 1954 State Championship.

MOPO LIFE: DREAM BIG. WRITE DOWN YOUR GOALS AND WORK TO REACH THEM.

THE ROCKY SERIES (Rated PG – PG13): Starring Sylvester Stallone, this boxing drama begins with a low-life boxer who is given an opportunity to fight for the Heavy-Weight Championship of the World. Rocky is the heavy underdog yet finds a way to keep perspective, give his best, and eventually come out victorious. Rocky gives advice throughout: "It's not about how hard you hit. It's about how hard you get hit and keep moving forward – how much can you take and keep moving forward. That's how winning is done!"

MOPO LIFE: WORK HARD AND STAY WITH THE PROCESS. YOUR OPPORTUNITY WILL COME.

Answer the following questions:

WHAT IS YOUR FAVORITE MOVIE? _____

How does your movie relate to the MOPO (<u>M</u>AX <u>O</u>UT <u>P</u>AY <u>O</u>UT) LIFE?

_____

_____

What does it mean to you to be the salt of the earth?

_____

_____

List 2 ways you can be salt in your world?

    1. _____

    2. _____

How will you stay salty in a world that drains the salt out of you?

_____

_____

What compels you to show a great passion?

_____

_____

Make a list of things you want to be passionate about:

_____

_____

_____

_____

MOPO LIFE: IT'S GOING TO THE MOVIES AND HAVING TO REFILL YOUR POPCORN BEFORE THE MOVIE STARTS. MOPO THE DAY!

Ephesians 2:10

For we are His creation—created in Christ Jesus for good works, which God prepared ahead of time so that we should walk in them.

MOPO LIFE: IT'S ADDING EXTRA BUTTER AND SALT TO YOUR POPCORN. MOPO THE DAY!

Mark 9:50

Jesus said, "Salt is good, but if the salt should lose its flavor, how can you make it salty? Have salt among yourselves and be at peace with one another."

MOPO LIFE: IT'S GIVING YOUR BEST EFFORT EVERYDAY AT WORK! MOPO THE DAY!

Colossians 3:17

And whatever you do, in word or in deed, do everything in the name of the Lord Jesus, giving thanks to God the Father through Him.

MOPO LIFE: IT'S STAYING POSITIVE WHEN EVERYONE ELSE AROUND YOU IS BEING NEGATIVE. MOPO THE DAY!

Colossians 3:14

Above all, put on love—the perfect bond of unity.

MOPO LIFE: IT'S ENCOURAGING YOUR NEIGHBOR DURING A TOUGH TIME. MOPO THE DAY!

Colossians 3:12

Therefore, God's chosen ones, holy and loved, put on heartfelt compassion, kindness, humility, gentleness, and patience,

MOPO LIFE: IT'S PRAYING FOR YOUR ENEMY. MOPO THE DAY!

Proverbs 24:17

Don't gloat when your enemy falls,
And don't let your heart rejoice when he stumbles,

MOPO LIFE: IT'S GIVING MORE THAN YOU TAKE. MOPO THE DAY!

Malachi 3:10

Bring the full 10 percent into the storehouse so that there may be food in My house. Test Me in this way," says the Lord of Hosts. "See if I will not open the floodgates of heaven and pour out a blessing for you without measure."

MOPO LIFE: IT'S TEXTING YOUR HUSBAND/WIFE TO SEE HOW THEIR DAY IS GOING. MOPO THE DAY!

Colossians 3:18-19

Wives, be submissive to your husbands, as is fitting in the Lord.
Husbands, love your wives and don't become bitter against them.

MOPO LIFE: IT'S SHARING THE LOVE OF CHRIST WITH THE WORLD YOU ARE LIVING IN. MOPO THE DAY!

John 21:17

Jesus asked Peter the third time, "Simon, son of John, do you love Me?"
He said, "Lord, You know everything! You know that I love You."
"Feed My sheep," Jesus said.

MOPO LIFE: IT'S FORGIVING WHEN THE WORLD IS TELLING YOU TO GET EVEN. MOPO THE DAY!

Colossians 3:13

Just as the Lord has forgiven you, so also you must forgive.

MOPO LIFE: IT'S BUYING A MEAL FOR A COMPLETE STRANGER. MOPO THE DAY!

Proverbs 19:17

Kindness to the poor is a loan to the Lord,
And He will give a reward to the lender.

MOPO LIFE: IT'S INVITING YOUR NEIGHBOR TO A CHURCH FUNCTION. MOPO THE DAY!

Mark 16:15

Then Jesus said to them, "Go into all the world and preach the gospel to the whole creation.

MOPO LIFE: IT'S BUYING YOUR STUDENTS ICE CREAM SANDWICHES. MOPO THE DAY!

Matthew 5:16

In the same way, let your light shine before men, so that they may see your good works and give glory to your Father in heaven.

MOPO LIFE: IT'S TAKING CARE OF YOUR HUSBAND/ WIFE WHO IS FIGHTING CANCER DAY IN AND DAY OUT, REMEMBERING YOUR VOWS OF UNTIL DEATH DO US PART. MOPO THE DAY!

Ephesians 5:28-33

In the same way, husbands should love their wives as their own bodies. He who loves his wife loves himself. For no one ever hates his own flesh, but provides and cares for it, just as Christ does for the church, since we arc members of His body.

For this reason, a man will leave his father and mother and be joined to his wife, and the two will become one flesh.

This mystery is profound, but I am talking about Christ and the church. To sum up, each one is to love his wife as himself, and the wife is to respect her husband.

MOPO LIFE: IT'S TRANSPORTING YOUR KIDS TO THE NEXT ACTIVITY SO THEY CAN PARTICIPATE IN THE THINGS THEY ENJOY. MOPO THE DAY!

John 3:30

He (Jesus) must increase, but I must decrease.

MOPO LIFE: IT'S HUGGING YOUR TEENAGED BOY EACH DAY AND TELLING HIM YOU LOVE HIM. MOPO THE DAY!

Colossians 3:21

Fathers, do not exasperate your children, so they won't become discouraged.

MOPO STORY

The 4th grade boy did not think very highly of his artwork. All he knew was his art teacher was a very nice lady, who was always very positive and encouraged him to keep drawing. One day he received a letter in the mail that said, "Congratulations – You have WON 1st Prize in the 500 Arts Contest"

To his surprise, the art teacher had entered his work into the contest. This did wonders for his confidence and made him appreciate his art teacher.

MOPO THE DAY!

TESTIMONIALS

"Teaching choir helps me MAX OUT my music experience, but it really helps the students MAX OUT. In the advanced groups, we spend so many hours perfecting our songs and craft. The end result is stunning, and the students love it so much. It's so hard to describe the feeling you get when you finish a concert choir set – both me as the director and for the students. Any of my students can tell you some of their favorite memories are singing at the Madrigal Dinner, performing in finals at North Central near the end of our competition season, or performing at ISSMA State Finals. It's mostly about the sense of accomplishment after putting in so much time for something. It's also special because the music just takes you to a different place and allows you to feel something that you can't replicate anywhere else. That's such a huge PAY OUT for all of us!

I try to have this same approach to worship music. I play piano every week (MAX OUT) on the worship team at church, and it's a way for me to give back to God what He has bestowed upon me. I always hope that our team will motivate others at church to feel the same way my students do. I am so thankful for my life and what music has done for me. Sharing it with others is such a privilege, and I look forward to it every day! (PAY OUT)"

Jason Damron – Music Teacher Mooresville High School

"I MAX OUT music in my life by enjoying it, but not living for it. By faith, we allow the Spirit to work through it to point beyond the music to God himself. The PAY OUT is loving the Lord with all that I am."

Mark Proctor – Tech Director

MOPO MUSIC

Turn it up! Do you sing in the car? Sing in the shower? Sing when nobody else is around? Then you understand the importance of MOPO MUSIC in your life. Music has a way of cheering us up, stirring our emotions, changing our moods, and giving us an extra bounce in our step. So many good songs have been created to help us enjoy this roller coaster of a ride we are on called life. I believe God created music in the beginning of time because He knew how music can move within our soul, how music can bring us all together, and how music can be used to worship. In *Revelation 4:8*, scriptures says this about that the living creatures in heaven: "Day and night they never stop, singing: Holy, holy, holy, Lord God, the Almighty, who was, who is, and who is coming." I believe the Lord is giving us this time on earth to warm up our musical talents before joining in that chorus one day in Heaven. We get opportunities every day to **M**AX **O**UT our voices in preparation for Heaven (Ultimate **P**AY **O**UT).

Music has played a role throughout my life. I have good memories of my dad singing to country songs in the car growing up. I fondly recall my parents taking us Downtown Indianapolis for a live concert being played on the circle. There was nothing like warming up before every home basketball game with the #1 band in the state at Franklin Central High School (they won the State Fair Band Contest all 4 years I was at FC). There were the songs we would sing at Camp Olivet, a church camp. There were those trips to Dale Hollow Lake where we would listen to music while playing cards, swimming, and taking boat rides. Music got me through piles of homework in college and was the backdrop for dances and other social gatherings. In each of these experiences, music played a significant role in making for a better life experience (**P**AY **O**UT).

The MO (**M**AX **O**UT) in the Music Experience is…

- o   taking time to listen to music in your day.
- o   singing out loud in the car, in the shower, wherever you are.
- o   lifting your voice up to the Lord in preparation for Heaven.
- o   dancing to your favorite song by yourself, with your significant other, or with friends.

The PO (**P**AY **O**UT) in the Music Experience is…

- o   cheering us up, stirring our souls, giving us a better perspective, and giving us a bounce in our step.
- o   helping to make our life experiences more memorable; for example, what song did you dance to at your wedding? You are not likely to forget a moment like that.
- o   getting us ready for an at-bat in baseball, a game with the rhythm of the songs played before the game. (Quick story: At Hanover College, we had a warm up CD that I requested: *Rocking in the USA* by John Mellencamp. When this song came on during warm-ups, I would raise my level of enthusiasm. My teammates noticed this about halfway through the season, and they would get a kick out of watching me warm-up.)
- o   preparing us for Heaven.

There are many songs out there that can represent the MOPO (**M**AX **O**UT **P**AY **O**UT) way of Life. I have chosen 6 of my favorites:

"JUST ANOTHER DAY IN PARADISE" by PHIL VASSAR

For those of you who have kids, this song highlights the challenges you go through as you raise your family (**M**AX **O**UT). The days are long, but the years are short. You find joy in making it through each day, and when you do, you ask yourself, "How did we do that?" You find the Lord provides and you find your paradise (**P**AY **O**UT).

Lyrics from the song:

It's just another day in paradise.
We'll there's no place I'd rather be
We'll it's two hearts, And one dream
I wouldn't trade for anything
And I ask the Lord, every night
For just another day in paradise.

MOPOLIFE: IT'S FINDING ENJOYMENT IN THE LITTLE THINGS.

"SUMMERTIME" by KENNY CHESNEY

No one looks forward more to the summertime than a school teacher. You have given your heart and soul to your kiddos all year long (**M**AX **O**UT), and now it's time for some fun in the sun (**P**AY **O**UT). You look forward to not being on a schedule, hanging with friends and family, going swimming, and grilling out with a beverage in hand. You look forward to the summertime!

Lyrics from the song:

Schools out and nights roll in
Man just like a long lost friend
You ain't seen in a while
You can't help but smile

It's a smile, It's a kiss
It's a sip of wine
It's the summertime
Sweet summertime

MOPO LIFE: IT'S HAVING FUN IN THE SUN WITH YOUR FRIENDS AND A DRINK IN YOUR HAND.

"STEAL MY SHOW" by TOBY MAC

Every day, each one of us is living out a show (**M**AX **O**UT). Who is in control of your show? Is it you, or is it the LORD? God wants you to yield control of your show. He wants you to let go and let God take control. He will bless you and allow you to bless others (**P**AY **O**UT).

Lyrics from the song:

No matter who we are
No matter what we do
Every day we can choose
If You want to steal my show,
I'll sit back and watch You go
If You got somethin' to say,
Go on and take it away
Need You to steal my show,

MOPO LIFE: IT'S LETTING GO AND LETTING GOD TAKE CONTROL OF YOUR LIFE. TRUST HIM.

"SHAKE A TAIL FEATHER" by THE FIVE DU-TONES

In *The Blues Brothers*, a classic '80s movie starring John Belushi and Dan Aykroyd, Ray Charles joins in to sing "Shake a Tail Feather." Do you ever feel like dancing – just letting go and shaking your body (**M**AX **O**UT)? This song will make you shake it. You will dance freely and have fun doing it. This song will put a smile on your face (**P**AY **O**UT).

Lyrics from the song:

Ahhhh!
Twist it

Shake it
Here we go loop de loop
Shake it up baby
Here we go loop de la
Bend over let me see you shake a tailfeather
Bend over let me see you shake a tailfeather

MOPO LIFE: IT'S BENDING OVER & SHAKING YOUR TAIL FEATHER.

"DO EVERYTHING" by STEVEN CURTIS CHAPMAN

Every day is a blessing. Each day gives us a clean slate to live the life God has called us to live – to be in tune with the Holy Spirit, to be a light in your home and your neighborhood, and to share the love of Christ with those you come into contact (**M**AX **O**UT). The (**P**AY **O**UT) is knowing that in sharing those experiences on earth with the people in your life, you will be sharing more experiences together in heaven someday.

Lyrics from the song:

As you do everything you do to the glory of the One who made you
Cause He made you to do
Every little thing that you do
To bring a smile to His face
And tell the story of grace
With every move that you make
And every little thing you do

MOPO LIFE: LIVE FOR CHRIST.

"I HOPE YOU DANCE" by LEE ANN WOMACK

Time to slow the songs down. Grab your partner and hold them close (**M**AX **O**UT). Enjoy the time together and the memory being made (**P**AY **O**UT). Oh, and don't forget to DANCE!

Lyrics from the song:

I hope you still feel small when you stand beside the ocean
Whenever one door closes I hope one more opens
Promise me you'll give faith a fighting chance
And when you get the choice to sit it out or dance
I hope you dance

MOPO LIFE: KEEP DANCIN!

What is your MOPO (**M**AX **O**UT **P**AY **O**UT) SONG in life?

_____

Asked another way, what is the song you would play for yourself before taking a swing at home plate (your walk-up song☺)?

_____

How has music played a role in your life?

_____

_____

How do you MAX OUT music in your life?

_____

_____

What is the **P**AY **O**UT for you when listening to your favorite music?

_____

_____

God has told us in the Bible that when we get to Heaven, music will be used to worship Him. What is your favorite MOPO worship song?

_____

What song do you look forward to singing in Heaven for the Lord?

_____

MOPO LIFE: IT'S TURNING UP THE RADIO IN THE CAR AND SINGING LIKE NO ONE IS WATCHING. MOPO THE DAY!

Psalm 9:2

I will rejoice and boast about You;
I will sing about Your name, Most High.

MOPO LIFE: IT'S DANCING WITH YOUR SON/DAUGHTER ON THEIR WEDDING NIGHT. MOPO THE DAY!

Psalm 7:17

I will thank the Lord for His righteousness;
I will sing about the name of the Lord, the Most High.

MOPO LIFE: IT'S SINGING IN THE SHOWER. MOPO THE DAY!

Psalm 47:6

Sing praise to God, sing praise;
Sing praise to our King, sing praise!

MOPO LIFE: IT'S SINGING AND DANCING HAND IN HAND WITH YOUR 6-YEAR OLD DAUGHTER. MOPO THE DAY!

1 Chronicles 13:8

David and all of Isreal were celebrating with all their might before God with songs and with lyres, harps, tambourines, cymbals, and trumpets.

MOPO LIFE: IT'S DANCING WITH YOUR WIFE TO YOUR WEDDING SONG. MOPO THE DAY!

Song of Songs 2:2

Like a lily among thorns,
So is my darling among the young women,

MOPO LIFE: IT'S STANDING IN CHURCH, SINGING OUT YOUR FAVORITE HYMN TO GOD. MOPO THE DAY!

Acts 16:25

About midnight Paul and Silas were praying and singing hymns to God, and the prisoners were listening to them.

MOPO LIFE: IT'S SINGING A LULLABY TO YOUR NEWBORN BABY AT TWO IN THE MORNING. MOPO THE DAY!

Zephaniah 3:17

The Lord your God is among you,
A warrior who saves.
He will rejoice over you with gladness.
He will bring you quietness with His love.
He will delight over you with loud singing.

MOPO LIFE: IT'S SINGING SONGS AROUND THE CAMPFIRE. MOPO THE DAY!

1 Chronicles 16:23

Sing to the Lord, all the earth.
Proclaim His salvation from day to day.

MOPO LIFE: IT'S MAKING A SONG MIX AND LISTENING TO IT ON THE BOAT RIDE. MOPO THE DAY!

Psalm 96:1

Sing a new song to the Lord;
Sing to the Lord, all the earth.

MOPO LIFE: IT'S LISTENING TO "EYE OF THE TIGER" WHILE YOU JOG ON THE TREADMILL. MOPO THE DAY!

Luke 1:37

"For nothing will be impossible with God."

MOPO LIFE: IT'S PICKING OUT THE PERFECT RINGTONE SONG FOR YOUR FAVORITE PEOPLE PROGRAMMED IN YOUR PHONE. MOPO THE DAY!

Exodus 15:2
The Lord is my strength and my song;
He has become my salvation.
This is my God, and I will praise Him,
My father's God, and I will exalt Him.

MOPO LIFE: IT'S SINGING KARAOKE WITH CONFIDENCE IN FRONT OF A CROWD. MOPO THE DAY!

Psalm 57:7

My heart is confident, God, my heart is confident.
I will sing; I will sing praises.

MOPO STORY

He was turning twenty-five, and his friends were taking him out to eat. He had requested a burger for his birthday. The place they chose had a 'Burger Challenge' – one would have to eat two pounds of meat with all the fixins to get a free meal: cheese, lettuce, tomato, onion, ketchup, mustard, mayo, and pickle. After some man-up challenges given by his buddies, he decided to take on the challenge. His meal was paid for.

MOPO THE DAY!

TESTIMONIALS

"I *MAX OUT* on my birthday by spending time with my family & friends. Celebrating another birthday means I've gotten to experience another year of competing, loving, teaching, & learning. The *PAY OUT* for me is knowing that the experience I have gained will help me conquer the challenges ahead & thrive in the days to come."

Kyle Brewer, Teacher/Basketball Coach/My Big Brother

"I *MAX OUT* my birthday by spending time with friends. The *PAY OUT* is growing deeper in my relationships & a joyful heart as we celebrate doing life together."

Mandi Uhlrich, Mom of Three Girls

In 2019, my son Luke and I were able to SERVE on a mission trip with a group from Plainfield Christian Church. We traveled to Kosova to run a Sports Camp and share the love of Jesus Christ with over a hundred elementary to high school aged kids. Stepping out of your comfort zone and experiencing God's Holy Spirit at work is an unforgettable MOPO Experience. MOPO the Day!

MOPO YOUR BIRTHDAY

Blow out the candles! It only happens once a year: a day dedicated to you living out 365 days of the year. Some people celebrate it while others try to ignore it. In my eyes, it's a special day; it's your MOPO DAY! God made this individual day for you. In *Jeremiah 1:5* it says, "I chose you before I formed you in the womb; I set you apart before you were born." These are the words spoken to Jeremiah. I believe these same words apply to our lives today. God created us before we entered the womb and set us apart to be part of His kingdom. It's up to you to make that individual decision. Your MOPO DAY is something to be celebrated!

If you are fortunate enough to have kids, you know the joy in the eyes of a five-year old when his birthday is coming up. And what do we do for the little guy? We throw him a party! We eat cake. We play games. We invite friends and family over. We open presents. Simply put, we CELEBRATE! Often times, we celebrate for days.

God gave us each a special day to celebrate the creation He made in His image – to evaluate our lives and to remind us of the blessing given to us each year. <u>His time is a gift</u>.

How are you using it, and how do you celebrate it? My suggestion? Celebrate your MOPO BIRTHDAY this year. Go out to eat. Blow out a candle. Hang with family and friends. Go on a trip. Do something you enjoy!

The MO (**M**AX **O**UT) in your Birthday Experience is…

- o   planning a fun day to celebrate.
- o   accepting you are another year older.
- o   taking time to be thankful for your blessings.

The PO (**P**AY **O**UT) in your Birthday Experience is…

- o   being with friends and family.
- o   getting presents from loved ones.
- o   doing something you enjoy.
- o   adding one to your age – another year of wisdom.

Answer the following questions:

If you could do anything on your birthday this year, what would it be?

_____

_____

Make a list of the people you want to celebrate your birthday with:

_____

_____

_____

_____

When God made you, what do you think He set out for you to do?

_____

_____

When the Bible says, "He made you in His image," what does that mean to you?

_____

_____

List 3 things you are THANKFUL for this year:

1. _____
2. _____
3. _____

MOPO LIFE: IT'S BLOWING OUT ALL THE CANDLES. MOPO THE DAY!

Proverbs 9:10

The fear of the Lord is the beginning of wisdom, and the knowledge of the Holy One is understanding.

MOPO LIFE: IT'S SENDING BIRTHDAY WISHES TO A FRIEND. MOPO THE DAY!

3 John 1:2

Dear friend, I pray that you may prosper in every way and be in good health, just as your soul prospers.

MOPO LIFE: IT'S CELEBRATING BECOMING A TEENAGER! MOPO THE DAY!

Psalm 90:12

Teach us to number our days carefully so that we may develop wisdom in our hearts.

MOPO LIFE: IT'S GETTING YOUR FIRST CAR AT SIXTEEN. MOPO THE DAY!

Psalm 20:4

May He give you what your heart desires and fulfill your whole purpose.

MOPO LIFE: IT'S TURNING EIGHTEEN AND BEING ABLE TO VOTE AND BUY LOTTERY TICKETS. MOPO THE DAY!

John 8:36

Therefore if the Son sets you free, you really will be free.

MOPO LIFE: IT'S HAVING YOUR FIRST BEER ON YOUR 21ST BIRTHDAY. MOPO THE DAY!

1 Peter 5:8

Be sober! Be on the alert! Your adversary the Devil is prowling around like a roaring lion, looking for anyone he can devour.

MOPO LIFE: IT'S CELEBRATING THE BIG 4-0! MOPO THE DAY!

Job 8:21

He will yet fill your mouth with laughter and your lips with a shout of joy.

MOPO LIFE: IT'S REMEMBERING WHO CREATED YOU. MOPO THE DAY!

Hebrews 11:3

By faith we understand that the universe was created by the word of God, so that what is seen has been made from things that are not visible.

MOPO LIFE: IT'S KEEPING PERSPECTIVE: THIS LIFE IS A MARATHON, NOT A SPRINT. ENJOY THE RIDE! MOPO THE DAY!

Ecclesiastes 3:1-8

There is an occasion for everything,
& a time for every activity under heaven:
A time to give birth & a time to die;
A time to plant & a time to uproot;
A time to kill & a time to heal;
A time to tear down & a time to build;
A time to weep & a time to laugh;
A time to mourn & a time to dance;
A time to throw stones & a time to gather stones;

A time to embrace & a time to avoid embracing;
A time to search & a time to count as lost;
A time to keep & a time to sew;
A time to be silent & a time to speak;
A time to love & a time to hate;
A time for war & a time for peace.

MOPO LIFE: IT'S TURNING 65 AND COUNTING YOUR BLESSINGS. MOPO THE DAY!

Psalm 103:2

My soul, praise the Lord,
And do not forget all His benefits.

MOPO LIFE: IT'S LIVING TO BE 100 SURROUNDED BY YOUR FAMILY. MOPO THE DAY!

Proverbs 9:11

For by Wisdom your days will be many, and years will be added to your life.

MOPO LIFE: IT'S CHERISHING EVERY MOMENT. MOPO THE DAY!

John 20:19

In the evening of the first day of the week, the disciples were gathered together with the doors locked because of their fear of the Jews. Then Jesus came, stood among them, and said to them, "Peace to you!"

MOPO LIFE: IT'S CELEBRATING YOUR BIRTHDAY FOR THE ENTIRE MONTH. MOPO THE DAY!

Psalm 118:24

This is the day the Lord has made;
Let us rejoice and be glad in it.

MOPO STORY

She was a 16-year-old high school student who had been in an automobile accident. The doctors told her that she would not walk again. Her body was broken, but her spirit was very much alive. She spent hours wrestling with God about being able to walk again. Her family would get her the help she needed and be her support system. As she began her rehab, she would hear the words of her grandfather saying, "Take one day at a time." The days were rough, and the road would be long. After three years of tears, hard work, grit, determination, and desire, she would walk again.

MOPO THE DAY!

TESTIMONIALS

"Any time I start to feel anxious, I believe it is an alarm that is prompting me to pray. I *MAX OUT* my anxieties by first naming the anxieties to the Lord and then it helps to visibly think of Him taking them off of my shoulders and putting them in the palm of His hand.

Many times the Lord will lead me to this verse (Philippians 4:8),

"And now, dear brothers and sisters, one final thing. Fix your thoughts on what is true, and honorable, and right, and pure, and lovely, and admirable. Think about things that are excellent and worthy of praise."

If I am thinking of things that are not true and noble, then I ask Him to remove them from my mind. One *PAY OUT* the Lord blesses me with is He reminds me of the ways He has sustained me the countless other times I worried. This is humbling and faith giving. He says remember when you were tired and I gave you rest? Remember how I sustained your son through heart surgery? Remember how your house finally sold? Remember how I gave you peace and comfort in your grief? Remember how I brought you a friend when you were alone? Remember how I restored a relationship that was broken? Remember how I died to save you from your sins and fears? Remember how I created the heavens and the earth? Remember child, keep remembering . . . and that's how I MOPO my anxieties."

Anissa Steinborn, Campus Leader at Multi-Site Church

When I am anxious I try to give those anxieties up to the Lord. He doesn't want us to be anxious or worries. Philippians 4:6 says, "Do not be anxious about anything, but in everything by prayer and supplication with thanksgiving let your requests be made known to God."

I *MAX OUT* by putting all of my trust in God to help me through those challenging situations. I fully believe He is in control. My *PAY OUT* is a peacefulness and confidence in knowing that my Holy & Loving Father hears me and will provide what I need\. It may not be the outcome I want, but I fully surrender to His will because He knows what is best for me.

Adam Guthrie, ESL Teacher

MOPO YOUR ANXIETY

Take a Breath! Turn the news on. What do you hear? All the problems of our world: viruses, people getting shot, people losing their jobs, bad weather. We live in a world where these thoughts can overtake our mind. What do we do about it? MOPO (**M**AX **O**UT **P**ASS **O**UT) your anxiety. What does that mean? **M**AX **O**UT your positive thoughts and **P**ASS **O**UT the negative ones. For example, I'm going to take a negative situation – let's say the COVID-19 – that has overtaken our world. Instead of living in fear of getting the virus, I'm going to think about the positive things going on in my life. I have a roof over my head. I have good health. My family is healthy and safe. I can spend time with my family. Getting COVID is somewhat out of my control when I'm living life. I understand I must do my best to stay indoors and not be around people, but I won't let the COVID-19 control my life. That's not living my best MOPO LIFE!

The MO (**M**AX **O**UT) in the MOPO (**M**AX **O**UT **P**ASS **O**UT) ANXIETY Experience is…

- o thinking of positive thoughts.
- o remembering the many blessings in your life.
- o controlling the things you can control.
- o trusting in knowing God is ultimately in control.

The PO (PASS OUT) in the MOPO (MAX OUT PASS OUT) ANXIETY Experience is…

o   putting your negative thoughts to rest.
o   writing out your anxieties on a piece of paper and giving them to the Lord in prayer.
o   taking a break from the news and negative social media.

MOPO LIFE is taking control of your thoughts and living out your best life. The Bible says:

> "Do not be anxious about anything, but in every situation, by prayer & petition, with thanksgiving, present your requests to God. And the peace of God, which transcends all understanding, will guard your hearts and your minds in Christ Jesus." Philippians 4:6-7

> "Cast all your anxiety on Him because He cares for you. 1 Peter 5:7

> "Anxiety weighs down the heart, but a kind word cheers it up." Proverbs 12:25

MOPO (**M**AX **O**UT **P**ASS **O**UT) your anxiety - - **M**AX **O**UT your positive thoughts so you can **P**ASS **O**UT your anxiety - - now you can MOPO the Day!

Make a list of the MOPO ANXIETIES in your life.

_____

_____

_____

_____

Time to make those things **PASS **O**UT.**

Take time to lift your MOPO ANXIETIES in prayer to the Lord. Do that now.

Make a list of the many blessings you have in your life.

_____

_____

_____

_____

Take time to THANK GOD for these blessings.

Time to **M**AX **O**UT these blessings with a thankful attitude.

MOPO LIFE: IT'S DOING A CANNON BALL OFF THE HIGH DIVE. MOPO THE DAY!

Deuteronomy 31:6

Be strong and courageous; don't be terrified or afraid of them. For it is the Lord your God who goes with you; He will not leave you or forsake you."

MOPO LIFE: IT'S WAITING FOR THE CHUTE TO OPEN WHILE SKY DIVING. MOPO THE DAY!

Revelation 14:6-7

Then I saw another angel flying in mid-heaven, having the eternal gospel to announce to the inhabitants of the earth---to every nation, tribe, language, & people. He spoke with a loud voice: "Fear God and give Him glory, because the hour of His judgement has come. Worship the Maker of heaven & earth, the sea & springs of water."

MOPO LIFE: IT'S KEEPING BOTH HANDS UP ON THE ROLLER COASTER. MOPO THE DAY!

Romans 12:2

Do not be conformed to this age, but be transformed by the renewing of your mind, so that you may discern what is the good, pleasing, & perfect will of God.

MOPO LIFE: IT'S TEACHING YOUR 15-YEAR OLD HOW TO DRIVE. MOPO THE DAY!

Romans 1:17

For in it (the gospel) God's righteousness is revealed from faith to faith, just as it is written: the righteous will live by faith.

MOPO LIFE: IT'S SENDING YOUR KID OFF TO COLLEGE. MOPO THE DAY!

Acts 13:2-3

As they were ministering to the Lord & fasting, the Holy Spirit said, "Set apart for Me Barnabas & Saul for the work that I have called them to." Then, after they had fasted, prayed, & laid hands on them, they sent them off.

MOPO LIFE: IT'S WALKING YOUR DAUGHTER DOWN THE WEDDING AISLE. MOPO THE DAY!

Proverbs 31:10-12

Who can find a capable wife?
She is far more precious than jewels.

The heart of her husband trusts in her,
And he will not lack anything good.
She rewards him with good, not evil, all the days of her life.

MOPO LIFE: IT'S GETTING DOWN ON ONE KNEE TO POP THE QUESTION: "WILL YOU MARRY ME?" MOPO THE DAY!

Genesis 1:27-28

So God created man in His own image;
He created him in the image of God;
He created them male and female.
God blessed them, and God said to them, "Be fruitful, multiply, fill the earth, and subdue it.

MOPO LIFE: IT'S HAVING A BABY FOR THE FIRST TIME. MOPO THE DAY!

Genesis 9:11

"I confirm My covenant with you that never again will all flesh be wiped out by the waters of a deluge; there will never again be a deluge to destroy the earth."

MOPO LIFE: IT'S TAKING A TEST WORTH OVER HALF YOUR GRADE. MOPO THE DAY!

James 1:2-3

Consider it a great joy, my brothers, whenever you experience various trials, knowing that the testing of your faith produces endurance.

MOPO LIFE: IT'S GOING FOR YOUR FIRST JOB INTERVIEW. MOPO THE DAY!

Joshua 1:7

Above all, be strong & courageous to carefully observe the whole instruction My servant Moses commanded you. Do not turn from it to the right or the left, so that you will have success wherever you go.

MOPO LIFE: IT'S PREPARING FOR A BIG GAME. MOPO THE DAY!

Romans 12:4-8

Now as we have many parts in one body, & all the parts do not have the same function, in the same way we who are many are one body in Christ & individually members of one another. According to the grace given to us, we have different gifts:

If prophecy, use it according to the standard of faith;
If service, in service; if teaching, in teaching;
If exhorting, in exhortation; giving, with generosity;
Leading, with diligence; showing mercy, with cheerfulness.

MOPO LIFE: IT'S GETTING ON A PLANE FOR THE FIRST TIME. MOPO THE DAY!

Hebrews 11:3

By faith we understand that the universe was created by the word of God, so that what is seen has been made from things that are not visible.

MOPO LIFE: IT'S TRUSTING AND OBEYING WHEN THE WORLD AROUND YOU IS IN CHOAS. MOPO THE DAY!

Ezekial 36:24-28

"I will take you from the nations & gather you from all the countries; then I will bring you to your land. I will sprinkle you with pure water & you will be clean from all your idols. I will give you a new heart, & I will put a new spirit within you. I will remove the heart of stone from your body & give you a heart of flesh. I will put my Spirit within you; I will take the initiative & you will obey my statutes & carefully observe my regulations. Then you will live in the land I gave to your fathers; you will be my people, & I will be your God."

MOPO STORY

He was a standout high school basketball player and straight A student. He wanted to continue his playing days and decided to go to a Division III school. He arrived on campus in August and quickly began learning how to navigate the college life. It was early mornings and late nights studying for his classes, with basketball practices in between. He didn't start on his TEAM right away. It was a spot that would have to be earned. With many ups and downs, he never lost faith in his ability. He stayed with the process and stayed committed to getting better every day. He would get his chance and his hard work would pay off.

MOPO THE DAY!

MY TESTIMONY

My name is Oggy Brewer. I'm a husband to Beth, a father to Luke, Olivia, Mallory and Kellen, a school teacher, a high school basketball coach, founder of MOPO, and a disciple of Christ.

What does it mean to be a disciple of Christ? It means *I have taken Jesus Christ as my Lord and Savior*, and every day I try to grow in my relationship with Him through prayer, serving others, reading the Bible, growing in relationship with other people, and trying to stay connected to Jesus.

I've always considered myself to be a good person. In high school, I was surrounded by some really good coaches who taught me many life lessons. Coach Mark James was my varsity basketball coach, and Coach John Rockey was my assistant-varsity basketball coach. Coach Rockey invited me and my siblings to Church Camp at Camp Olivet. It was here where my faith started to grow, and I accepted Jesus as my Lord and Savior. I would go on to be baptized as a sophomore in high school.

I continue to be a work in progress. With this COVID-19 affecting each one of us, God has opened my eyes to the many idols that I have allowed to be in my life: sports, work, and the busy-ness of life. These things are all good things, but I realize I have consumed my world with such things and rooted God out of parts of my heart. While these times have brought their own challenges, I'm thankful to God for His continued patience with me and our world in bringing our focus back to Him.

Jesus said, "*I am the way, the truth, & the life - - No one comes to the Father accept through Me.*"

I have total faith in knowing God is in control of these times. It is in this faith that I have a peace that can only come from Jesus.

WRITE OUT YOUR TESTIMONY:

_____

_____

_____

_____

_____

_____

_____

_____

_____

_____

_____

_____

_____

_____

_____

_____

_____

THE ULTIMATE MOPO MEANING

After having read my testimony, I'd like to share with you the ultimate MOPO (**M**AX **O**UT **P**AY **O**UT) meaning. Each of us is given one life on this earth; it is up to us how we use it. While I've encouraged you to **M**AX **O**UT each day so you can have a **P**AY **O**UT, the reality is each of us have a decision we need to make: TO FOLLOW JESUS OR NOT? All of us will eventually **M**AX **O**UT **P**ASS **O**UT when our life on earth is over. The ultimate **M**AX **O**UT **P**AY **O**UT will be when you accept Jesus as your Lord and Savior and meet Him face to face in Heaven. Jesus says in *Revelation 22:12-13*, "Look! I am coming quickly, and My reward is with Me to repay each person according to what he has done. I am the Alpha and the Omega, the First and the Last, the Beginning and the End."

If you choose to accept Jesus as your Lord and Savior, take a moment to offer up this prayer:

Dear God,

I know that my sin has come between You and me. I know that I need a Savior. I acknowledge that JESUS is that Savior. Thank You for sending Jesus to die on the cross in my place – that He raised to life on the third day, and that You offer me forgiveness of my sins and eternal life with my belief in Him. I accept JESUS now, trust that ALL my sins are forgiven, and accept this invitation to live eternally in Heaven with You.

Thank You, JESUS!

In JESUS' name, AMEN.

Here's to making that decision to follow JESUS and to celebrating knowing you have the ultimate MOPO (**M**AX **O**UT **P**AY **O**UT) coming!

After giving your life to Jesus, The Bible tells us two very important things happen now. Number one, we become His sons and daughters, members of His family forever. Number two, God Himself comes into our lives and takes residence within our hearts by His Spirit. Congratulations! You have made the most important decision of your life! You now belong to God, and He lives within you! Thanks to Jesus for taking away our sins! AMEN!

You now start the ultimate MOPO relationship with God.

Feel free to reach out to me if you want to talk further about this relationship, share a MOPO story in your own life, or have any questions or comments. (mopo4life@yahoo.com)

If you are already a believer, I want to encourage you to continue to fight the good fight. **KEEP RUNNING THE RACE**. We are in this together, and keep faith in knowing JESUS has already walked amongst us, died on the cross, and rose again. He will be back.

We will all meet again in Heaven and have a MOPO (**M**AX **O**UT **P**AY **O**UT) party with Jesus!

THANK YOU'S

As I think about this book and the many people who have helped shape my thoughts to make me the person I am today, I'd like to take this time to THANK these people:

Rick and Sara Brewer – My parents have always taught me to give my best, treat people with respect, and to always finish what you start (3rd grade football☺).

Kyle and Brittany Brewer – My siblings taught me how to share and care for one another.

Beth Brewer – My wife continues to teach me how to love unconditionally and grow in our Christian walk through prayer, serving others, and raising our family. I LOVE YOU!

Luke, Olivia, Mallory, and Kellen Brewer – My kiddos continue to teach me humility and how important it is to laugh each day. Thankful to be your Dad!

Grand Ma and Pa Craig – My grandparents, who walked with the Lord daily, showed me unconditional love.

My PFF's – You have taught me the importance of having friends to lean on, grow with, and cry on as I do life. Very thankful for these friendships.

These Coaches have played a significant role in my life:

Chuck Stephens – He was Franklin Central's Varsity Football Coach when I was growing up; he allowed me to be the ball boy of the varsity football TEAM. I got to experience what it was like to be around a WINNING coach.

John Mallory – He was Franklin Central's Varsity Football Coach when I was in high school; he met me in the weight room after school every day to help me get stronger. He held me accountable.

Craig Marks – He was on Franklin Central's Varsity Football Coaching Staff; he was also part of the weight program that helped me get stronger. He also held me accountable.

Mark James – My head high school varsity basketball coach taught me to compete hard, prepare well, and that you can only control the things you can control.

John Rockey – My assistant high school varsity basketball coach and youth director taught me the importance of making things fun, giving me confidence by holding the guards accountable each week and sharing the Gospel with me.

Mark Woodrow – My JV basketball coach taught me the importance of being patient with a freshman kid on the JV Team.

Rick Brewer – My 8th grade basketball coach and dad taught me the importance of always giving my best effort, doing things the right way, and setting goals to work towards achieving.

Jeff Butcher – My 7th grade basketball coach taught me to always bring joy and love to the game.

Cindy Huffman – My elementary Physical Education teacher and Middle School Tennis Coach. She taught me how to find enjoyment in physical exercise and taught me the skills of tennis.

Mike Raters – My high school tennis coach taught me how to compete in tennis at a higher level and that hard work is rewarded. LET'S GOOOO!

Mike Bietzel – My college basketball coach at Hanover for 2 years taught me the importance of holding people accountable and giving me confidence with his words.

Jon Miller – My assistant basketball coach at Hanover for 2 years taught me the importance of being relational and going into every game with a solid game plan to try to WIN.

Kyle Getter – My assistant basketball coach at Hanover for 2 years lived in a house with us and taught me the value of building friendships and having someone to talk to.

John Grimes – My college basketball coach at Marian College for 2 years taught me the importance of being patient with players and saying when you're open, MAKE IT!

Kyle Brewer – I coached with my brother for 4 years at South Putnam; he taught me the importance in building a program to make sure you are developing the younger kids.

Bob Carter – I have coached with him for 15+ years at Mooresville High School; he taught me to make the best of every situation, to love unconditionally, and everyone is valuable in the program.

Also, I want to give a shot out to all of my coaches – from Little League Baseball, Basketball, and Football – to strength coaches – to tennis coaches – each have had an impact in my life. THANK YOU!

A BIG THANKS to the Coaches, Teachers, Ministers, and Friends & Family who I reached out to and shared a **MOPO LIFE** anecdote.

A huge THANK YOU shout out to **Chris Stevenson** for editing the book.

<u>If you are a coach reading this, what an awesome responsibility you have in making a difference in a kid's life</u>. It may not always feel like you are having a huge impact right now, but years down the road, your kids will have a THANKFUL heart for the IMPACT and memories made while under your guidance. <u>Keep being a positive example,</u> and remember to **MOPO the DAY!**

Last Assignment:

1) List one person in your life (a parent, teacher, coach, minister, friend, neighbor) who has poured into you (_**M**AXED **O**UT_ their time & energy) and allowed you to experience a _**P**AY **O**UT_ in your life.

If you are able, give that person a call, text, or send an email or letter to say THANK YOU.

2) Now list one person who you want to pour your time & energy into (_**M**AX **O**UT_) so they can experience and pass on a _**P**AY **O**UT_ to others.

Lift up a prayer for God to use you and bless this relationship.

Blessings upon you as you live out the _**MOPO LIFE!**_

**Don't forget to visit the website: www.mopo4life.com**

**Twitter: MOPO4LIFE@BrewerOggy   #MOPOtheDAY!**

#MOPO4LIFE   #MOPO4LIFE   #MOPO4LIFE   #MOPO4LIFE